NEW JERSEY 9/11 MEMORIALS

NEW JERSEY
9/11 MEMORIALS

A Photographic Guide

Including the National Memorials

SEPTEMBER 11, 2001

"WE WILL REMEMBER"

Brian M. Holmes and Min Xie

Foreword by Thomas H. Kean, 9/11 Commission Chairman

First edition

Book Design by Brian M. Holmes

ISBN-13: 978-1477535097

ISBN-10: 1477535098

To all those who perished on September 11, 2001. You are remembered.

A portion of the profits of this book will fund New Jersey 9/11 Memorials.

Contents

Preface

September 11, 2001 is a day that will be remembered in the United States for decades to come, if not forever. The day that America was attacked by terrorists and nearly 3,000 innocent citizens and residents were murdered has been memorialized by the citizens of cities and towns all over the U.S., and indeed in many countries around the world. Unfortunately most individuals can't travel to visit each and every memorial, and that's a shame because many are fine works of art as well as heartfelt remembrances of loved ones.

New Jersey 9/11 Memorials – A Photographic Guide takes you to visit the many loving specimens created in New Jersey where September 11, 2001 was felt particularly hard. The book brings to you, in one place, dozens of beautiful color photographs along with pertinent background information about each memorial. The photographs and information gathered in this book may inspire the reader to go out on his or her own journey to visit local memorials, or just appreciate them within the book's pages. In addition, *New Jersey 9/11 Memorials* includes the historical background and timeline information concerning the terrorist attacks and the responses in the ensuing years, as well as a chapter including the names of every victim of the terrorist act.

Unfortunately, this book cannot contain all the 9/11 memorials conceived and built in the world, the U.S., or even just in New Jersey where there are more than 200 physical memorials to the victims and rescue workers of the attacks.

Never before has a book brought together so many September 11 memorials and monuments and information about them in one place so that the reader can participate in (and meditate on) the honoring of the victims by each affected community of the worst terrorist attack ever against the American people. It is humbly hoped that *New Jersey 9/11 Memorials – A Photographic Guide* will spread awareness of these beautiful and heart-felt tributes and contribute to the everlasting preservation of remembrances of the lives of our lost brothers and sisters in the terrorist attacks of 2001. As the National September 11 Memorial and Museum in New York City states on a wall near the victims' remains, "No Day Shall Erase You from the Memory of Time". This is the object of every 9/11 memorial, and the object of *New Jersey 9/11 Memorials – A Photographic Guide*.

A portion of the profits from this book will fund unfinished memorials in the state of New Jersey.

Foreword

There are certain events that change our world – the great depression, the two world wars, the dropping of the first atomic bomb. We were never the same again.

Such an event was the September 11 attack on the World Trade Center. It changed history. As a direct result we have been engaged in two of the longest wars in our history. Paying for these wars has resulted in a large deficit and an increasingly fragile economy.

On a personal level we find air travel has become a nightmare, photo ID's are required to get into buildings, our driver's licenses have changed, and for the first time in 200 years, we are nervous about our safety in our own country.

All this was caused by 19 men who entered this country illegally, evaded every defense this country had and created more devastation than the Japanese attack on Pearl Harbor. For the first time since the war of 1812 there was a successful attack on the soil of the continental U.S.

We responded in a number of ways. We created a huge bureaucratic agency and named it the Department of Homeland Security. We announced that we would declare war on any country that harbored those who had plotted the attack. When Congress' own committee failed to investigate the plot to the satisfaction of the American people, the families of the 9-11 attack lobbied successfully for the creation of a bipartisan committee which I chaired to get to the bottom of how and why this happened and to lessen the chance of it ever happening again. That was the 9-11 Commission which resulted in the largest intelligence reform in U.S. history.

As the shock started to wear off the stories emerged. Tragic stories of individuals, the tales of heroism on that day and the strength of those who survived. I have never known a braver group of people than the families of 9-11. Out of the tragedy rose this extraordinary group dedicated first to insuring that they got the full story of the plot and how it had been allowed to happen and second to ensure that policies were put in place so that this would never happen ever again. As members of the Commission we called the families of 9-11 "the wind in our sail" as they supported our efforts to get the whole truth and helped us push for the 41 recommendations to make us all safer.

At home in our towns the shock was terrible. New Jersey lost only a few less people than New York. If you lived or worked as I did in a suburban community, you knew people who had been in those towers or on those planes. I went to funerals for six months as families decided when and how to remember their loved ones. I remember speaking at one such service and seeing pregnant women in the front row, children soon to be born who would never know their fathers. In the local railroad stations vacant cars remained for weeks awaiting owners who never again would get off the train.

People started asking – How shall we remember our loss? How can we build something so our loved ones can be remembered? How can we memorialize our community loss?

In New York, the memorial and museum were placed on the site of the Twin Towers. In New Jersey, a simple but beautiful memorial rose at Liberty State Park – but that was not enough. Each town wanted to do something special to remember their own.

Town meetings were held, private and public funds were solicited. Families were consulted and ground was broken and memorials started to rise. They are extraordinary in their diversity and their beauty, each town trying its best to tell future generations how they felt that day and how they wanted to remember their loved ones. Some are designed by artists, some by scholars, some by children, they tell the story.

This book contains many of these memorials. As we look at these designs and read the inscriptions we are brought back to that tragic day. We remember once again the victims and those brave people who rushed into the buildings to save them. In these monuments we once again remember best and the worst of that day. The diversity is wonderful. Each community expresses its loss in a different way. Each recalls the story for its children and grandchildren. Each tells us in their own way that we must never ever forget those loved ones who we lost that clear September morning. As many of the monuments remind us, it's about "remembrance and rebirth".

Thomas H. Kean,

June 22, 2012

(*Thomas Kean was the 48th governor of New Jersey (1982-1990). Following his popular governorship, Kean served for fifteen years as the president of Drew University in Madison, NJ. Governor Kean was the 9/11 Commission Chairman, which investigated the September 11, 2001, attacks on the U.S. He was appointed to the post by President George W. Bush.*)

Acknowledgements

Thank you to my wife Min Xie for her invaluable help with the photography and photo editing, and for her forbearance with my lack of employment throughout much of the production of this book. I am lucky to have found such a patient and loving wife who shares so many interests with me.

I would also like to thank the people around me, co-workers, friends and family, for encouraging me in my desire to see through this endeavor. Producing a book isn't all sunshine and Applebee's, and sometimes, when the inevitable walls and closed doors present themselves, we all need a little reinvigoration of our drive.

I would also like to acknowledge Napoleon Hill, Angela Booth, and John Locke for their inspirational writing. These three writers motivated me over the course of this book's production.

Introduction

On the morning of September 11, 2001, I was on my way to work, as was the rest of the United States' east coast. The September sky in New Jersey was a brilliant blue with literally not a cloud in sight. The leaves were only just getting ready to change color and were still two or three weeks from falling. The summer humidity was gone and the temperature was seasonably warm for 8:45 in the morning. I was in my car driving alongside the Earle Naval Weapons Station on Route 34's long, straight, fenced-in stretch through that base. (The public highway bisects the naval base for three or four miles.)

I was listening to a New York City morning radio personality, someone who was always good for a laugh or two on the way to work. Not long after 8:47 a.m., his producer came on the air and said that an airplane had hit one of towers of the World Trade Center. The information was sketchy and the authorities and media weren't even sure what kind of plane it was (i.e., whether it was a small single engine plane or what). It was literally moments since it had happened. But the radio host was already speculating about Osama bin Ladin being behind it, and so was I. I don't remember if I had made it to work before the second plane hit. But when that happened, there was no doubt in anyone's mind that this was no accident. I was stunned and so were my co-workers. To a great extent, that day changed every day which followed it for Americans and the world.

After the second passenger jet hit the South tower of the World Trade Center, the day was largely a wasted work day. People were looking for news reports on the Internet, streaming news reports, watching the events on the TV in the cafeteria, and listening to radios. There were quiet, shocked discussions amongst employees. Soon other planes hit the Pentagon, and a Pennsylvania field and speculation at work was running wild. Would this keep happening all day long? Then, after burning for more than an hour, the World Trade Center towers fell. For hours we were waiting for more planes to hit more targets. The airspace over the United States was shut down in an effort to prevent any more possible terrorist acts, and orders were given to shoot down any plane not following Federal Aviation Administration (FAA) instructions. President Bush appeared to be missing in action.

The Damaged Pentagon

On that morning there was question as to whether United Flight 93, which went down in a Shanksville, Pennsylvania field, was shot down. We found out later in the day that it wasn't. Instead there was heroism on that plane. Heroism and sacrifice which cost the hero passengers of that flight their lives, but which may have saved hundreds of other lives, and prevented the destruction of yet another symbol of America, the White House or the United States Congress.

Crash at Shanksville, PA

There were heroes on United Flight 93, and there were heroes at the World Trade Center in New York City and at The Pentagon in Washington D.C. And President Bush did arrive back in Washington D.C. later that day and in the evening spoke to the nation and the world about the terrible event.

The 3000 people who died on September 11, 2001 and the heroes that saved lives that day have had memorials erected in their honor all over the United States of America. New York, New Jersey, Pennsylvania, Connecticut, Washington D.C., and more, are all host to hundreds of these tangible remembrances. But the memorials are also found in many additional states, and even in other countries. Some are made of granite, steel, or brass. Many incorporate trees and other living things into the memorial's design. Many are benches, or gardens, or memorial flagpoles. There is a wide range of creativity displayed in all of these tributes. The one thing they all have in common is that they were conceived with reverence and love for innocent and/or brave fellow citizens and family members.

In the pages which follow, my co-photographer Min Xie and I present as many of these New Jersey memorials as space will allow in a reasonably sized book. But because of the constraints of full-color book publishing, not every New Jersey memorial can be included in these pages. (There are over two hundred permanent New Jersey September 11 memorials.) Despite this we were able to get 86 September 11 memorials included in the pages of the book along with the four national September 11 memorials which, although they are not in New Jersey we felt were too important to leave out of a book presenting 9/11 memorials. The four "national" memorials we included are three of them run by the federal government (the World Trade Center memorial, The Pentagon memorial, and the Shanksville memorial) and one in

Boston at Boston Logan International airport which is included because of the fact that two of the hijacked planes took off from there.

The average person will only be able to see a handful of memorials in their everyday life. Perhaps at the train station in their own town, or at a park in a nearby town. In fact, getting out and seeing the memorial in your own town (if it has one) is something that everyone should do, especially on September 11 when there are usually special memorial services taking place. But one should also remember that the memorials placed in our town squares are there to be viewed at any time, and should be. It is one more thing which connects us to our communities, and fellow Americans.

There are so many beautiful and reverent September 11 memorials in New Jersey that it is a shame they do not have wider appreciation. Min and I wanted to see as many as we could and share them with you.

That is the purpose of this book. To honor the lives of the heroes and victims of September 11 by giving their memorials a larger audience. *New Jersey 9/11 Memorials – A Photographic Guide* allows you to see and appreciate memorials that you may never get to see for yourself in person. You can participate in the reverence, honor, and beauty of each 9/11 memorial without having to drive miles to see it. And if you want to head out on the road to see a few New Jersey memorials *New Jersey 9/11 Memorials* can make that easier too.

If you do decide to go out and see many of the memorials yourself you will not be disappointed. The project of traveling to the many various townships, towns, and boroughs portrayed in the pages of this book has been an edifying and enjoyable one. In a lot of ways New Jersey IS America. There are quaint, small towns and busy large ones, typical American Main Streets, and a surprising number of farms, forests, mountains, beaches, and swamps. There are also unpleasant areas and extremely pleasant ones, as well as office parks, national parks, state parks, county parks, and city parks. The only geographical features we didn't see in our New Jersey travels were glaciers and deserts. Other than these, the diminutive state of New Jersey has a little bit of everything to offer geographically. The journey to discover the September 11 memorials of New Jersey has been a journey of discovery of a fine state as well. This was helped in no small way by TomTom and Garmin GPSs, which made finding all these far flung memorials so much easier than it would have been.

New Jersey 9/11 Memorials starts out with beautiful, high resolution, color photographs of each 9/11 memorial. This is accompanied by information (if space allows) such as what material it's made of, the memorial's designers, and the inscriptions on or near the monuments. Along with this, if space allows, there is also location information such as cross streets or addresses.

The inscriptions on monuments of individual victim names and donors to memorials were not transcribed to their respective memorial pages within this book due to space constraints. However, the names of all of the people who died as a result of the tragedy that day are included in this book in the Victims of September 11, 2001 chapter.

September 11, 2001 is a tragic day that all Americans wish had never happened. We came together in shock and determination as a country that day, in a way that we rarely do. Even now, more than ten years later, many of those responsible are still being hunted. In May 2011, nearly ten years after the worst act of terrorism ever committed, Osama bin Ladin, the impetus behind the attacks and al Qaeda was finally brought to justice when U.S. forces tracked him down to his hideout in Pakistan and killed him. The U.S. and much of the world sighed with relief and joy that the recent embodiment of evil in the world had been finally dealt with. September 11 "mastermind" Khalid Sheik Mohammed's trial began only in May of 2012, even though he had been in custody since 2003.

Every day brings new attempts by al Qaeda and its supporters to kill vulnerable, innocent civilians wherever in the world they can. The fight begun more than ten years ago by al Qaeda goes on. Evil acts perpetrated on freedom-loving people continue on a daily basis. The U.S. and other governments continue to hound, hunt, capture, and/or kill al Qaeda terrorists all over the world. Unfortunately there seems to be no decrease in the terrorist's efforts.

It is my hope that this book, *New Jersey 9/11 Memorials – A Photographic Guide,* will be part of the national effort to always remember a day when the United States of America was attacked by evil people, and when the world realized that Osama bin Ladin and other Islamic extremists were engaged in a war against it, a war which must be fought until good people win over a cowardly, disillusioned, and evil ideology.

Please enjoy *New Jersey 9/11 Memorials* and remember the heroes of that day. As the National September 11 Memorial and Museum states on a wall near the victims' remains,

"No Day Shall Erase You from the Memory of Time"

The Story of 9/11

Before 9/11

The story of 9/11 is not just the story of what happened on the day of September 11, 2001, although the events of that day are extremely important and have changed the way Americans interact with the world. The story of 9/11 is also rooted in the context of events which happened over the previous 25 or 30 years leading up to that terrible day. That history is long and complicated and not suited to a photographical book. Some of the important events are touched on here. For an in-depth background into the historical context leading up to 9/11 you can refer to *The 9/11 Commission Report*, which tells the story very well.

1978 The Soviet Union invades Afghanistan in an attempt to buttress a failing Marxist Afghan government against Islamic rebels.

1979 Iran's Shah, Mohammed Reza Pahlavi, was overthrown in an Islamic Revolution leading to the rule of a fundamentalist Islamic republic by the Ayatollah Ruhollah Khomeini.

1979 Iranian "students" storm the U.S. embassy in Tehran taking 66 people hostage in a hostage crisis that lasts 444 days. President Carter loses his re-election bid in part because of his inability to resolve the crisis. The hostages are freed on President Reagan's inauguration day.

Ayatollah Khomeini

1980s The United States and other nations decide to help the rebels (Mujahideen) in Afghanistan by supplying weapons and training to fight the Soviet troops. Osama bin Ladin is among those Mujahideen, mainly providing his money and leadership.

Iraq and Iran are at war with each other for most of the 1980s. President Saddam Hussein of Iraq uses nerve gas during the war with Iran and at the end of the war against the Kurds in northern Iraq, killing 5,000 people, and debilitating 10,000 more.

1983 A Hezbollah bomb explodes killing 241 U.S. Marines in their barracks during a peacekeeping mission in Lebanon. President Reagan pulls the Marines out of Lebanon in response, making the U.S. appear weak.

Iranians Showing Support for Hostage-taking

1988 A bomb explodes on a U.S. bound Pan Am 747 resulting in the deaths of 271 people in Lockerbie, Scotland. Libya later acknowledges responsibility for the bombing.

1989 After nearly a decade of fighting, the Soviet Union comes to see the futility of its involvement in Afghanistan and decides to leave the country. The Soviets and the U.S. agree not to interfere in Afghanistan's politics or government. However, weapons continue to flow in to both sides of the Afghan political conflict.

1990 Iraq invades Kuwait because Kuwait would not forgive Iraq's war debt from the Iran-Iraq War.

1991 A military coalition of thirty countries with the United States as the leader is assembled by President George H.W. Bush and through a long bombing campaign and short invasion by ground troops, evicts Iraq from Kuwait. Saudi Arabia allows coalition forces to use bases in its country. This is a point of great distress to the Saudi native Osama bin Ladin and his followers.

The Soviet Union is formally dissolved after nearly seventy years of oppressive rule.

1993 The first bombing of the World Trade Center. Six people are killed and 1,000 people are injured. Investigated and tried as a criminal act by the Clinton administration.

American helicopters are shot down in Somalia leading to U.S. withdrawal from that dysfunctional, war-torn African "nation". While there is good reason to question why we are there in the first place, the withdrawal of the troops by President Clinton again is a blow to perceived U.S. military prowess.

1995 A car bomb explodes in Riyadh outside a joint Saudi-U.S. facility for training Saudi national guard. Five Americans and two Indians are killed. Saudi Arabia quickly finds and executes some suspects without giving American officials a chance to interrogate and investigate the suspects' guilt.

The Alfred P. Murrah Federal building in Oklahoma City, Oklahoma is bombed by anti-government extremists Timothy McVeigh and Terry Nichols killing 168 people and injuring hundreds of other people.

1996 Osama Bin Laden leaves Sudan where he'd lived since being run out of Saudi Arabia. Now he is persona non grata in Sudan and he sets up shop in Afghanistan where he forges an alliance with the Taliban. With a lot of weapons and a power vacuum in the country, much of Afghanistan is taken over in 1996 by the extremist Islamic group. The Taliban is a repressive, backwards, intolerant, and ruthless sect bent on subordinating women, and destroying the people and cultures of other religions, and imposing their harsh brand of Sharia Islamic law. The Taliban give bin Ladin free reign to create al Qaeda jihadist training bases in Afghanistan.

A large truck bomb explodes in the Khobar Towers residential buildings in Dhahran, Saudi Arabia killing 19

Americans and wounding 372 people.

1998 Osama bin Laden, Ayman al Zawahiri, and others publish a fatwa (Islamic religious proclamation) in a London newspaper which called for the murder of any American, anywhere on earth, as the "individual duty for every Muslim who can do it in any country in which it is possible to do it."

Simultaneous bombings at U.S. embassies in Nairobi, Kenya and Dar es Salaam, Tanzania. The attack on the U.S. embassy in Nairobi killed 213 people, just 12 of whom were Americans, most of the rest of the dead being Kenyans. About 5,000 people were injured. The attack on the U.S. embassy in Tanzania killed 11 more people but no Americans.

U.S. demands extradition of Osama bin Ladin and the Taliban refuses. Cruise missiles are fired into Afghanistan to destroy terrorist training bases run by Osama bin Ladin in response to the embassy bombings.

1999 Training begins for the operatives who would become the terrorist hijackers in al Qaeda's "Planes Operation."

2000 The USS Cole is rammed by a 35-foot boat laden with explosives and two suicide bombers on board while the battleship is refueling at a port on the coast of Yemen. Seventeen Navy crewman are killed and 47 injured.

The first operatives in al Qaeda's Planes Operation arrive in the United States.

Cruise Missile Launch

9/11

On the morning of September 11, 2001, the United States is attacked by terrorists using four fully-fueled passenger airliners as weapons of mass destruction and sacrificing the lives of hundreds of people on those planes as they were crashed at more than 500 miles per hour into the World Trade Center towers, the Pentagon, and a field in Pennsylvania. The actions of the passengers of United Flight 93, informed as they were by the other hijackings and crashes, minimized the potential for more death and destruction through their heroic actions to abort the terrorists' plot to fly the last plane into the U.S. Capitol or White House. The attacks killed nearly 3,000 people from 93 nations.

6:45-7:40 a.m. In Boston, Mohammed Atta, Abdul Aziz al Omari, Satam al Suqami, Wail al Shehri, and Waleed al Shehri board American Airlines Flight 11 bound for Los Angeles.

7:25 In Boston, Marwan al Shehhi, Fayez Banihammad, Mohand al Shehri, Ahmed al Ghamdi, and Hamza al Ghamdi board United Airlines Flight 175 bound for Los Angeles.

7:30-7:50 At Washington D.C.'s Dulles International Airport, Khalid al Mihdhar, Majed Moqed, Hani Hanjour, Nawaf al Hazmi, and Salem al Hazmi board American Airlines Flight 77 bound for Los Angeles.

7:40 At Newark International Airport, Saeed al Ghamdi, Ahmed al Nami, Ahmad al Haznawi, and Ziad Jarrah board United Airlines Flight 93 bound for Los Angeles.

7:59 American Airlines Flight 11 takes off from Boston's Logan Airport.

8:14 United Airlines Flight 175 takes off from Boston's Logan Airport.

8:15 American Airlines Flight 11 hijacking begins to take place.

8:20 American Airlines Flight 77 takes off from Washington Dulles International Airport.

8:42 United Airlines Flight 93 takes off from Newark International Airport.

8:43 United Airlines Flight 175 hijacking begins to take place.

8:46 American Airlines Flight 11 crashes into the North Tower of the World Trade Center.

8:51 American Airlines Flight 77 hijacking begins to take place.

9:03 United Airlines Flight 175 crashes into the South Tower of the World Trade Center.

9:25 All civilian air traffic in the United States is ordered grounded.

9:28 United Airlines Flight 93 hijacking begins to take place.

9:37 American Airlines Flight 77 crashes into the Pentagon.

9:59 The South Tower of the World Trade Center collapses.

10:03 United Airlines Flight 93 crashes into a field in Shanksville, Pennsylvania.

10:28 The North Tower of the World Trade Center collapses.

5:21 p.m. The 7 World Trade Center building collapses from damage sustained from the Twin Towers collapses.

8:30 President Bush addresses the nation from the White House concerning the attack on the U.S.

After 9/11

9/13/2001 Planes are once more allowed to fly as the national airspace is reopened to civilian air traffic.

9/17/2001 The U.S. financial markets reopen.

9/20/2001 President Bush addresses the nation before a joint session of Congress, gives the Taliban an ultimatum, and draws America's line in the sand against terrorism. "We will make no distinction between the terrorists who committed these acts and those who harbor them."

9/22/2001 Office of Homeland Security formed.

10/7/2001 The first military airstrikes occur against the Taliban in Afghanistan.

10/26/2001 The Patriot Act, an intelligence gathering and sharing law, is signed by the President.

11/13/2001 The Taliban flee Kabul, the capital of Afghanistan as opposition forces like the Northern Alliance and an increasing number of U.S. troops begin to gain control of Afghanistan's major urban areas.

5/30/2002 The last of piece of WTC steel is ceremonially removed from Ground Zero.

11/2002 Department of Homeland Security formed by an act of Congress.

2003 Khalid Sheikh Mohammed (KSM), mastermind and manager of the 9/11 plot is captured. He began his extremist career as a member of the Muslim Brotherhood in Kuwait before coming to North Carolina to earn his bachelor's degree in mechanical engineering.

In an effort to contain President Saddam Hussein and prevent his use of suspected weapons of mass destruction, the U.S. and other countries invade Iraq beginning a bloody eight-year war and occupation.

2004 The publication of *The 9/11 Commission Report*.

2006 Preliminary work begins One World Trade Center (Freedom Tower).

Former President Saddam Hussein is tried by an interim Iraqi government and hanged for his crimes against humanity.

9/11/2008 Pentagon September 11 memorial dedicated.

5/1/2011 Osama bin Ladin is killed in a raid on his compound in Pakistan, where he has been living for years, by a special team of U.S. forces.

9/10/2011 The 9/11 memorials at the World Trade Center, Shanksville Pennsylvania, and at Liberty State Park, New Jersey are dedicated and open to the public.

5/5/2012 Military tribunal of Khalid Sheikh Mohammed and four other top al Qaeda terrorists begins at the military base at Guantanamo Bay, Cuba.

2013 Rising up from the site of the 2001 terrorist attacks, the new One World Trade Center is complete.

World Trade Center Tribute in Light

The National Memorials

National 9/11 Memorial at the World Trade Center, New York City

New York, New York

The National September 11 Memorial is a tribute of remembrance and honor to the nearly 3,000 people killed in the terror attacks of September 11, 2001 at the World Trade Center site, near Shanksville, Pennsylvania, and at the Pentagon, as well as the six people killed in the World Trade Center bombing in February 1993.

The Memorial's twin reflecting pools are each nearly an acre in size and feature the largest manmade waterfalls in the North America. The pools sit within the footprints where the Twin Towers once stood. Architect Michael Arad and landscape architect Peter Walker created the memorial design selected from a global design competition that included more than 5,200 entries from 63 nations.

The names of every person who died in the 2001 and 1993 attacks are inscribed into bronze panels edging the memorial pools, a powerful reminder of the largest loss of life resulting from a foreign attack on American soil and the greatest single loss of rescue personnel in American history. (*from www.911memorial.org*)

Dedicated: September 10, 2011

The construction of the September 11 museum, pictured here behind the north reflecting pool, was slated to be finished in 2012. The museum structure looks like a WTC building lying down on its side. It will commemorate the lives of every victim of the 1993 and 2001 attacks by telling their stories through photos, video, sound, artifacts, and words. The memorial's grounds (pictured below) are expansive, park-like and almost serene in the midst of busy downtown Manhattan. Security procedures just to get into the memorial rival that of a TSA shakedown at the airport. Be sure to reserve your free pass online many days before going to the memorial or you will not get in.

As can be seen in the photo on the next page, there is still ongoing construction all around the World Trade Center site. So entrance to and exit from the site is tightly controlled. There are many security personnel on site as well as park information guides ready with their iPads to answer memorial related questions.

We had seen pictures of the memorial prior to our visit, but were in no way prepared for the size and scale of its presentation.

Aerial view of the WTC memorial site, above; Names etched into bronze counter around the reflecting pools, below.

The Pentagon 9/11 Memorial

The Pentagon 9/11 Memorial

The National 9/11 Pentagon Memorial in Arlington County, Virginia preserves the memories of 184 lives extinguished by terrorists who slammed a fully fueled jet airliner into the Pentagon. The memorial consists of simple aerodynamic benches, each representing a victim of the attack, that give the feeling of flight and are lined up with the trajectory of American Airlines Flight 77 as it headed towards the building at 530 miles per hour. The benches that represent Pentagon deaths face one way and the benches that represent Flight 77 deaths face the other. They are also lined up by age from one side of the memorial park to the other. Each bench has its own reflecting pool of water and victims from the same family are linked together by a plaque at the end of the pool of water, which lists their family members who also died in the attack. The memorial was dedicated on September 11, 2008.

Inscription: We claim this ground in remembrance of the events of September 11, 2001. To honor the 184 people whose lives were lost, their families, and all who sacrifice that we may live in freedom. We will never forget.

Inscriptions: We will be forever grateful to the thousands of people from across the nation and around the world who contributed their time, resources and energy to create this Memorial.

On September 11, 2001, acts of terrorism took the lives of the thousands at the World Trade Center in New York City, in a grassy field in Shanksville, Pennsylvania and here at the Pentagon. We will forever remember our loved ones, friends and colleagues.

Flight 93 National Memorial, Shanksville, Pennsylvania

Flight 93 National Memorial, Shanksville, Pennsylvania

Phase 1 of the Flight 93 National Memorial is complete. Depending on funding, it is anticipated that phase 2 will be done by 2014 and phase 3 after that. However, there is enough to see and revere if you go now – as much, or more in fact than many "complete" memorials. There is the Memorial Plaza and its marble wall with the 40 names of the passengers and crew of United Flight 93 inscribed upon it. The Memorial wall follows the path of Flight 93 as it headed towards its crash. There is also a visitor's center where you can sign a visitor's book and look at a timeline of events and read other information. National Park Service rangers are on hand to assist and answer questions. It is worth the trip into the beautiful hinterlands of Pennsylvania.

Dedicated: September 10, 2011

Special Info: Our visit was also very windy and bitterly cold for September, perhaps due to the altitude of this place. So go dressed for the weather if it's between September and May. While you're in Somerset County, Pennsylvania, go and visit the architect Frank Lloyd Wright's Falling Water House. It's not far and is worth the trip. But call ahead as the tours sell out ahead of time.

Flight 93 National Memorial, Shanksville, Pennsylvania

Site of the crash of Flight 93, above and below left;   Visitor center, below right

Boston Logan International Airport, Boston, Massachusetts

Boston Logan International Airport, Boston Massachusetts

The 9/11 memorial at Boston Logan International Airport is one of the most beautiful and most unusual 9/11 memorials in the U.S. The memorial site consists of an inscripted plaza with seating, a reflective pathway, and a large glass sculpture that features two glass panels etched with the names of the passengers and crew of each flight which took off from that airport to crash into the World Trade Center. This memorial is not easy to find or see unless you are specifically on a hunt to see it, or if you are staying at the hotel across the parking lot from it. Even if you are taking a flight somewhere from this airport, it is not something that you'd just come across very easily. It's almost as if it has been sequestered somewhere. Add to this the fact that nowhere at the memorial does it speak of what the events were that should be "remembered". It is worth finding if you are in Boston though.

Dedicated: September 9, 2008

Inscription: Remember this Day. This memorial is intended as a place of reflection for all those who were forever changed by the events of September 11, 2001.

Special Info: American Airlines Flight 11 and United Airlines Flight 175, the airplanes used by the terrorists as weapons of mass destruction to bring down the World Trade Center, took off from Boston at 7:59 a.m. and 8:14 a.m.

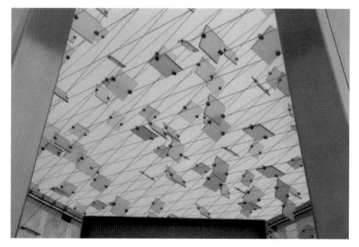

Suspended Glass Panel Roof

Boston's Logan International Airport, Boston Massachusetts

The New Jersey Memorials

Allendale, New Jersey

Allendale, New Jersey

The Allendale September 11 memorial is located at Crestwood Pond in Crestwood Park next to the red barn. The park is on West Crescent Avenue. It was designed by Jason Delabruyere, a sophomore in college and Emily Roshler, a sixth grader at the time. The memorial consists of the granite monument with a bronze flying eagle and a draped American flag. There are also two granite memorial benches and many inscribed pavers make up the pentagon-shaped plaza.

Inscription: 9-11-01 Time changes the heart, but the heart never forgets the memories within. We Remember

Atlantic Highlands, New Jersey

Atlantic Highlands, New Jersey

The Friends of Monmouth County 9/11 Memorial is another memorial with a "birds-eye" view of the distant Manhattan skyline. A marble eagle flies over a pentagonal pedestal while gripping a twisted steel beam from the WTC wreckage. The names of the residents of Monmouth County lost on that day are inscribed into the granite pedestal. The sidewalk leading up to the plaza and monument displays a timeline of the events.

Inscription: On September 11, 2001, many came to this site to witness the horrific tragedy just a few miles away in lower Manhattan. And for days afterward, they continued to come to view the smoke spiraling up from the site, most still in shock, not believing what they were seeing. From their beginning, the World Trade Center towers dominated the view from here. Through the years, many have come to visit this site and enjoy the view. Now, the towers no longer in view, we still picture them in our mind. And while we do, we remember a loved one, a relative, a friend, a neighbor, a co-worker, an acquaintance we lost that day. At the same time, we also remember where we were when tragedy struck and how our lives changed…forever. On July 22, 2002, The Monmouth County Board of Chosen Freeholders charged a committee of interested citizens with the task of designing and constructing a memorial to the 147 citizens of Monmouth County lost on that tragic day. The Monmouth County 9/11 Memorial Committee along with the friends of Monmouth County Park system completed this task three years later. On September 11, 2005, the memorial was officially dedicated.

Bayonne, New Jersey

Bayonne, New Jersey

The Monument to the Struggle Against World Terrorism was a gift from the people of Russia. It is a very difficult memorial to find, being off the beaten path in the Port of Bayonne. Even a GPS won't help you find it. But it is worth going to see for its sheer size and uniqueness. It faces the World Trade Center's location across Upper New York Bay. The base of the large memorial is inscribed with all of the names of those lost in the tragedy on that day. There is a smaller memorial in the park devoted to the people from Bayonne who died that day as well as a piece of steel from the destroyed buildings.

Inscriptions: Harbor View 9/11 Memorial Park Dedicated September 11, 2007.

In Remembrance of the Bayonne Residents Who Lost Their Lives in the Terrorist Attacks on Our Country on February 26, 1993 and September 11, 2001.

Gift from the People of Russia President Vladimir Putin * Monument to the Struggle Against World Terrorism * Artist Zurab Tsereteli

Berkeley Heights, New Jersey

Berkeley Heights, New Jersey

Located at 211 Park Avenue, the Berkeley Heights 9/11 Memorial Park consists of a twisted steel beam from the World Trade Center, a dedication monument, plaque, and flagpole, in a landscaped park with benches.

Inscription: Dedicated to the memories of the Residents of Berkeley Heights Who Lost Their Lives On September 11, 2001. With Gratitude to the Police Officers, Fire Fighters, Emergency Services Providers, and Civilians Who Unselfishly Gave of Themselves During This Terrible Tragedy.

Bernards, New Jersey

The Bernards September 11 memorial is located in Harry Dunham Park at 490 Somerville Road. The memorial consists of a circular tiled plaza with memorial pavers, a circular bronze plate with the names of some of the victims of the tragedy, steel from the fallen World Trade Center, benches, a flagpole, and landscaping in and around the plaza.

Inscriptions: A Place To Remember. A tribute to life, lives lost and lives changed forever. September 11, 2001

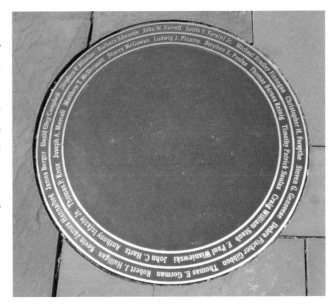

Bordentown, New Jersey

Two small reminders in beautiful downtown Bordentown.

Brick Township, New Jersey

IN MEMORY OF
BRETT T. BAILEY

JIM SANDS JR

Brick Township, New Jersey

"Angel in Anguish" is the name of Brick Township's September 11 memorial and was created by local artist Brian P. Hanlon who also created the impressive Pennsauken 9/11 memorial shown in this book. It is located at Windward Beach Park on Princeton Avenue. This memorial was originally dedicated in 2002 and rededicated in 2010. The metal sculpture remembers eight Brick residents who died in the tragedy that day.

Chatham, New Jersey

The Chatham Fire Department 9/11 memorial is a simple but uniquely designed memorial on the Firehouse Plaza in Chatham, near the police station and not far from the train station. It consists of a steel beam from the World Trade Center placed inside a steel circle with a representation of the Earth affixed to it. There is also a dedication plaque on the monument's pedestal.

Dedicated: September 11, 2004

Inscription: Dedicated to ALL who gave their lives on September 11, 2001 including our Brother Firefighters, Police & EMS. Their Sacrifice is our Loss. Their Courage is our Strength. Guiding the World towards a Brighter Future. Chatham Fire Department September 11, 2004.

Chatham, New Jersey

Chatham, New Jersey

The Chatham 9/11 Memorial Garden is located at 214 Main Street behind Chatham's public library.

Inscriptions: Welcome to the 9/11 Memorial Garden. Dedicated to our hometown neighbors, families and friends who lost their lives on September 11, 2001. May you find solace in this garden. "What we once enjoyed and deeply love we can never lose, for all that we love deeply becomes a part of us." – *Helen Keller* Dedicated: September 7, 2008

This Memorial consists of two beams from the World Trade Center Towers. They are placed North and South, 9 feet 11 inches apart and stand 9 feet 11 inches tall in remembrance of the date. The white doves in flight symbolize mankind's spirit, peace and love. Seven doves were chosen to acknowledge the 7 year anniversary. The circular placement of the name plaques is to signify there being no beginning and no end. This garden contains many windows. Views that capture colors, shapes and sounds. Together they become moments of serenity and tranquility.

AS TWO NATIONS COLLIDE, WE STAND SIDE BY SIDE.
YOU MAY HAVE DESTROYED AN AMERICAN WONDER,
BUT OUR CRIES OF ANGER FILL THE AIR LIKE THUNDER.
AS WAR BREAKS ON ENEMY LAND,
HERE IN AMERICA OUR FLAG WILL STILL STAND.
THE FLAG REPRESENTS FREEDOM,
IT WILL STILL WAVE IN THE TIME THAT WILL COME.
AS LOST SOULS MAKE THEIR WAY TO HEAVEN,
WE WILL NEVER FORGET SEPTEMBER ELEVEN.
- TAMMY GRAHAM

"SERVICE ABOVE SELF"
DEDICATED
TOWNSHIP OF CLARK
SAL BONACC   , MAYOR

JAMES A. NELSON
JULY 10, 1961 TO SEPTEMBER 11, 2001

Clark, New Jersey

The James Nelson Memorial Park is located at Grand Street and Broadway. The Memorial consists of a laser-etched granite monument, in a small landscaped park with flagpoles and a couple benches.

Clifton, New Jersey

Clifton, New Jersey

"One World United For Peace", a bronze sculpture by Michael Alfano is located at the Clifton Municipal Center at 900 Clifton Avenue near the entrance of the Arts Center.

Closter, New Jersey

Closter, New Jersey

The Closter September 11 memorial is located in Memorial Park on Harrington Avenue. It consists of a two piece granite monument, one piece an arch representing a doorway and the other piece a wall with a hole cut into it that looks skyward. There are also four stone benches on the circular tiled plaza and the memorial is set in a nicely landscaped park with a stream running through the park just behind.

Inscription: September 11, 2001 * Let Our Grief Become Strength, Our Remembrance Hope, Our Unity an Enlightened Path Toward Peace

Colts Neck, New Jersey

Colts Neck, New Jersey

The Colts Neck September 11 Memorial Fountain and Garden was designed by sculptor and artist Jim Gary. It is located at the municipal center on 124 Cedar Drive. It consists of a metal sculpture of flowers and butterflies in a fountain surrounded by memorial benches, a piece of steel from the WTC, and an artistic plaque.

Inscription: So long as we live, they too shall live, For now they are a part of us, As We Remember Them. * The events of September 11, 2001, were tragic. Our nation lost thousands of innocent people. Our town lost five good men. This garden is a place to meditate and remember.

Cranford, New Jersey

The Cranford World Trade Center Memorial resides in Cranes Park at 8 Springfield Avenue at the intersection of North Union Avenue. The monument consists of six connected columns set in a semi-circle at the base of which is a plaque with the name of a Cranford resident who perished. The simple sentiment "Cranford Remembers * September 11, 2001" spans the six columns at the top. The memorial also contains a plaza, a bench, and landscaping including cherry trees which were in blossom when we were there.

Dedicated: September 11, 2003

Demarest, New Jersey

Demarest, New Jersey

The Demarest September 11 memorial is located at Demarest Duck Pond at County Road and Hardenburgh Avenue. It consists of a group of stones arranged in a roughly pentagonal fashion, two of which are standing to represent the Twin Towers, an I-beam from the WTC site, and a dedicatory plaque. It reminded us of Stonehenge in a way.

Inscription: We honor the memory of all the victims of the cowardly terrorist acts perpetrated on the United States on September 11, 2001. Let this memorial, with this I-beam from the World Trade Center, serve as a: Reminder … Lest We Forget, Tribute … To The Innocent Victims And Unselfish Rescue Workers, Symbol … Of Our Nation's Strength, Unity and Resolve. God Bless America. Dedicated by the residents of Demarest, NJ September 11, 2004.

Dover, New Jersey

The Dover September 11 memorial is located at Prospect and West Blackwell Streets. It consists of two steel beams from the World Trade Center and a carved wood replica of the Twin Towers.

Inscriptions: Carved from a Tulip Tree as a Memorial to all who Died 9-11-01. By Hudson Favell. Donated to The Town of Dover. Placed here 4-11-02

Dover Remembers

This memorial site is a dedication to those who lost their lives on September 11, 2001. They will never be forgotten. Dedicated September 11, 2002.

East Brunswick, New Jersey

East Brunswick, New Jersey

The East Brunswick 9/11 memorial depicts the Twin Towers of the World Trade Center and is wrapped in a laser-etched American flag. The names of eight East Brunswick residents lost in the tragedy are etched into the towers. It is located on a memorial grounds with other memorials in East Brunswick's municipal center at One Civic Center Drive. Designed by Blaise Batko who designed memorials in Old Bridge, South River, and Middlesex, NJ as well.

Inscription: Dedicated to the memory of the loved ones who perished in the World Trade Center disaster SEPTEMBER 11, 2001 They will live in our hearts and minds forever

East Rutherford, New Jersey

East Rutherford, New Jersey

The East Rutherford September 11 memorial is located at Park and Railroad Avenues across from the train station. The memorial consists of a fountain, a piece of steel recovered from the WTC, a representation of New York City's skyline with the Twin Towers shown as missing sections in the brick wall. There is also a memorial clock, brick benches, and a flagpole in the brick-paved plaza.

Inscriptions: In Remembrance of September 11, 2001. This piece of structural steel from the World Trade Center is dedicated to the memory of those who perished so tragically and honors those who responded so valiantly. "We shall draw from the heart of suffering itself the means of inspiration and survival" – Sir Winston Churchill * September 11, 2011

On this date our nation was attacked by a group of terrorists. Their depraved act of hatred took the lives of thousands of innocent Americans including four of East Rutherford's own. * Our lives will be forever changed by this cowardly attack on our nation. This monument, dedicated to those members of our community who were lost, is a testament to the American resolve to fight terrorism, tyranny and oppression. The names of our lost are forever engraved here; eternally etched into the walls of our hearts. We will always remember. We shall never forget.

Edison, New Jersey

Edison, New Jersey

Edison's September 11 memorial is located at Lake Papaianni Park near the municipal complex on Route 27. The paved plaza includes a fountain, benches, and a flagpole. There a number of names inscribed around the fountain. There are also pieces of the WTC buried on the site as attested by a small, inscribed marker stone at the base of the flagpole.

Inscriptions: Edison Remembers September 11, 2001

Symbolically buried here are pieces of steel and stone recovered from the World Trade Center

Elizabeth, New Jersey

The Elizabeth September 11 Memorial is located at the Midtown Train Station on 11 West Grand Street. It was designed by Dario Scholis and dedicated on September 10, 2002. The 8-foot tall granite monument consists of twin towers, a flag background, a clock with the time that the first plane hit the WTC carved into the stone, the date of the attack, and the names of six residents who died. The plaza has some landscaping as well as three flagpoles flying the U.S. flag behind the monument.

Fair Haven, New Jersey

Fair Haven, New Jersey

The Fair Haven September 11 Memorial is located at Veteran's Park at the intersection of Fair Haven Road and River Road. The memorial consists of a small circular plaza surrounded with bushes and trees, memorial benches, and a large urn on an inscribed granite pedestal.

Inscriptions: The Fair Haven September 11th Memorial is the physical symbol which serves as a remembrance of those who perished, were wounded, or affected by the events of September 11th, 2001, as well as a sign of the strength and resilience that Fair Haven residents, as Americans, have increasingly shown since that terrible day – Dedicated September 11th 2005

"Let them not depart from our eyes; keep them in the midst of our hearts." – Proverbs

Peace * Liberty * Freedom * Strength *Sacrifice * Faith * Hope * Honor

Freehold Borough, New Jersey

The Freehold Borough 9/11 memorial is a simple, small memorial at the municipal building in downtown Freehold, near the fire department and the train station. It consists of granite twin towers on a pentagonal granite base.

Inscriptions: In Memory of Those Lost 9/11/01 * Designed by Freehold Intermediate School Accelerated Class Grade 7 2001-2002 * Pentagon Washington D.C. * Somerset County, PA * World Trade Center New York, NY

Freehold Township, New Jersey

Freehold Township, New Jersey

The Freehold Township memorial is located at the municipal center on Municipal Plaza Rd. just off of County Route 537. The impressive memorial consists of a replica of the Twin Towers on a pentagonal base on a plaza with a plaque and benches.

Inscriptions: September 11, 2001 * American Flight 77 * United Flight 93 * United Flight 175 * American Flight 11

The towers before you are 9' 11" tall, set upon a circle of fifty gold stars representing the United States. This circle "Ground Zero," rests upon the Pentagon, four sides of which have been engraved with the flights that were lost on September 11th. Interred in the foundation of the monument are pieces of steel from the World Trade Center, a symbolic resting place for thousands of unidentified victims. Mountain Laurel, the Pennsylvania state flower, has been planted on site to honor the heroic efforts of the passengers of Flight 93.

Glen Rock, New Jersey

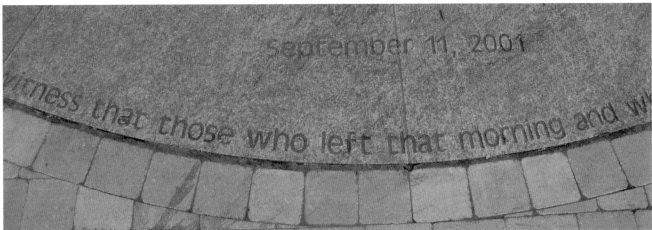

Glen Rock, New Jersey

The Glen Rock September 11 memorial is located at Main and Rodney streets near the train station. The memorial consists of a monument which has a shiny triangle in front of two matt-black rectangles. A steel beam from the WTC is hidden behind the monument as is a bench and a wall inscribed with the names of Glen Rock victims. There is also a flagpole, a circular plaza, and a walkway. The memorial is situated in a carefully landscaped area of a park.

Inscriptions: The steel I-beam that serves as the focus of the memorial is a gift from the City of New York to the Borough of Glen Rock in memory of our eleven Glen Rock residents lost on September 11, 2001, at the World Trade Center. It was recovered from the base of the North Tower eight days before the "Closing Ceremony" at Ground Zero on Wednesday, May 22, 2002.

The original piece measured approximately twenty-four feet as it ascended from the pit and was cut into a fourteen foot length for transport to New Jersey. One hundred and ten inches of its length stretch skyward from the floor in reference to the one hundred and ten stories of the World Trade Center Towers. The steel is anchored in a footing containing ashes recovered from Ground Zero.

Green Brook, New Jersey

Green Brook, New Jersey

Green Brook's September 11 memorial is located at Top of the World Park on Top of the World Way. The paved plaza includes a wall with eighteen plaques that include the names of all the 9/11 victims. Also included is a steel beam from the World Trade Center, a buried urn of ashes from Ground Zero, and some benches, flagpoles, and two encased posters showing the World Trade Center and the 9/11 timelines.

Inscription: Green Brook Township Memorial Tragically Lost Lovingly Remembered Dedicated September 11, 2005

Beneath this steel we laid to rest a measure of the ashes saved. Although the quantity is small, we hope this urn somehow contains the essence of the ones we lost God bless these poor remains.

Hamilton Township, New Jersey

Hamilton Township, New Jersey

The Hamilton Township 9/11 Memorial Grove is located within Hamilton Veterans Park. The grove includes some evergreen trees, a steel beam from the WTC, three dedication plaques, and a glass covered brick sarcophagus containing items from Ground Zero.

Inscriptions: To Our Heroes September 11, 2001 * This grove of evergreen trees is dedicated as a place of reflection in the memory of four citizens of Hamilton. They lost their lives in the terrorist attack on The World Trade Center buildings in New York on September 11, 2001. This grove is also dedicated to those citizens of Hamilton who served in the volunteer efforts associated with the tragedy. May each person who pauses here remember their sacrifice and their spirit. * We Will Always Remember, Let Us Never Forget. September 11, 2001. May this steel beam from the World Trade Center Towers stand as a lasting memory of the innocent lives we lost on September 11, 2001, and as an enduring tribute to the Police Officers, Firefighters and Emergency Responders who gave their lives to save others, and as a constant reminder of the brave members of the United States Armed Forces who defend our freedom and sometimes make the ultimate sacrifice. May this serve as a timeless memorial to this tragedy.

Harrison, New Jersey

Harrison, New Jersey

The Harrison September 11 memorial is located near the post office (427 Harrison Ave.) and library between 5th Street and Frank E. Rodgers Boulevard. The memorial consists of some large twisted pieces of structural steel from the WTC site. Water drips from the top of one of the beams making it a fountain of sorts. There is also a laser-etched granite monument with the official sentiment from the town, as well as five flagpoles and some benches in a landscaped, fenced-in corner of a park.

Inscriptions: Eternal Remembrance. It is with great sadness and heavy hearts, but with a strong resolve and belief, that we, as American Citizens, shall never forget the heinous and cowardly act of destruction and carnage that was perpetrated against our Nation and all the free world on Tuesday, September 11, 2001, that the Town of Harrison, NJ as a community, dedicates this memorial to all those who lost their lives in that horrific chronicle of evil. And with a loving remembrance of all the brave men and women, heroes all, who made the supreme sacrifice that day in the line of duty, with the hope that others might be saved.

Hazlet, New Jersey

The Hazlet September 11 memorial is located at Veteran's Park at 1776 Union Avenue. It is a black granite obelisk etched with the names and faces of Hazlet's lost residents and the emblems of the first responders. The landscaped plaza is made with memorial pavers and has polished granite memorial benches as well. There is also a small piece of steel from the WTC site.

Inscriptions: September 11, 2001 - A Moment in Time Now a day in History

If tears could build a stairway and memories were a lane I would walk right up to heaven to bring you home again. No farewell words were spoken no time to say goodbye you were gone before I knew it and only God knows why. My heart still aches in sadness and secret tears still flow what it meant to lose you no one will ever know – Anonymous

Highlands, New Jersey

Highlands, New Jersey

The Highlands September 11 memorial is located in Highlands Veterans Memorial Park (not far from Sandy Hook National Recreation Area) and consists of two large marble statues with male and female figures seemingly trying to free themselves of the rock. Encircling the statues there are also four large granite rocks with one side sanded flat and polished to a fine finish and inscribed with the names of those lost in the attacks of that day. Stephen Shaheen was the lead artist.

Holmdel, New Jersey

Holmdel, New Jersey

This memorial is a large round block of granite with two hands reaching out of it skyward. It is surrounded by a pentagon-shaped sidewalk on which are located polished granite benches. It's located on city hall property.

Dedicated: September 12, 2004

Monument Inscriptions: September 11, 2001. Freedom, Faith, Hope, Love, Family, Peace, Liberty, Heroism, Unity. United Flight 175, American Flight 77, American Flight 11, United Flight 93.

Plaque Inscription: The Holmdel September 11 memorial was dedicated on September 12, 2004 and erected to keep the Holmdel residents and family members lost in the attack on the World Trade Center forever in our hearts. The memorial is 9 feet tall and 11 feet wide and is made from 90,000 pounds of granite. The granite sidewalk depicts The Pentagon. The four flight numbers of the planes lost are displayed on the granite base along with inscriptions of all four service departments. The World Trade Center is hand etched on the face of the memorial, and the hands which were hand sculpted, are cast in bronze. Personal letters written by the families of those who perished are buried inside the memorial.

Hopatcong, New Jersey

Hopatcong's September 11 memorial is located in front of the borough hall at 111 River Styx Road. The memorial consists of a pentagonal granite obelisk on a pentagonal base. It is inscribed with sentiments, an image of the WTC, and a timeline of the day's tragedies. The monument is topped by some twisted metal and there are two steel beams from the WTC in the same yard which is also home to a fire fighter memorial.

Inscriptions: September 11, 2001 "We Will Never Forget" 2977 lives were lost, among them FDNY – 343, NYPD – 23, Port Authority PD – 37, EMS Personnel – 8. * Although the images of September 11, 2001 remain etched in our memory, we find solace in unity……a unity that rose from the ashes, restored faith in America's Indomitable Spirit and brought our Nation together. God Bless America

Howell, New Jersey

Howell, New Jersey

The New York skyline adorns the floor of the Howell September 11 memorial and five concrete arches meet at a pentagon keystone at the top of the monument representing the people who died at The Pentagon. The five pillars represent each person from Howell who died that day. On the pillars are etched symbols of America's freedom — the Twin Towers, the Statue of Liberty, and a bald eagle — as well as a plaque for each of the Howell men killed.

Within the monument is a boulder from Shanksville, Pennsylvania, where United Flight 93 crashed, and a piece of rusting steel from the World Trade Center. The memorial is at the Howell municipal complex at 251 Preventorium Road. It was designed by Miguel Eiras, and dedicated on October 28, 2005.

Inscription: America has stood down enemies before, and we will do so this time. None of us will ever forget this day, yet we go forward to defend freedom and all that is good and just in our world. – George W. Bush

United Airlines Flight 93 Crashes in Shanksville, PA. "They knew then that they were next and they decided to do something about it."

Howell, New Jersey Squankum Firehouse

Jersey City, New Jersey

Jersey City, New Jersey

There are three pieces to the September 11 memorial at the end of Grand Street on the Hudson River overlooking the World Trade Center site just across the river. The first is a pile of twisted steel beams, the second is a granite monument, and the third is a makeshift memorial made around a sculpture of a businessman sitting with a briefcase open on his lap. The sculpture by Seward Johnson was rescued from the rubble and set up amid the wreckage in NYC becoming a makeshift memorial. Now in Jersey City the sculpture still seems to be accruing sentiments.

Inscription: On the morning of September 11, 2001, these Jersey City residents were killed during the attack on the World Trade Center. This memorial is dedicated to those who died, those who survived, and those whose lives were changed forever on that day. * In loving memory of those who died on 9-11-01. We will always remember. Dedicated on 9-11-02, by the members of the 9-11 Memorial Committee of Jersey City, Inc.

Jersey City, New Jersey

Jersey City, New Jersey

A simple September 11 memorial in front of the Jersey City Fire Department First Division at 355 Newark Avenue using steel beams from the World Trade Center.

Jersey City, New Jersey

The Dauntless Efforts September 11 memorial sculpture is located at 5 Harborside Plaza near the ICAP September 11 Memorial.

Inscription: Dauntless Efforts by Matt Johnson. Dedicated to the memory of the victims of the September 11, 2001 attack on the World Trade Center. On September 11, 2001, construction workers at the Harborside Financial Center development sites rushed to the World Trade Center to donate their time, efforts and unique skills to the rescue and recovery efforts. This sculpture, depicting a silhouette of an iron worker amidst the wreckage or the World Trade Center, honors their heroic efforts. The steel used in the base of this sculpture is from the actual wreckage of the World Trade Center.

Jersey City, New Jersey

The ICAP September 11 Memorial is located at 5 Harborside Plaza near the Dauntless Efforts Iron Workers memorial. Each glass block contains the name of an employee who perished in the World Trade Center.

Inscription: September 11, 2001 * In Memory * Our Promise to Those Friends and Fellow Employees Who Perished on That Tragic Day Is That We Will Always Remember Them. Dedicated by the Employees of ICAP North America September 11, 2005

Keansburg, New Jersey

The Keansburg 9/11 memorial is really just an etched headstone depicting the Twin Towers and Tower 7 of the World Trade Center. There are also two concrete benches, a flagpole, and a couple of planters. It is located at the beach and near Keansburg's boardwalk. Despite being unassuming, it is the promise to remember that counts here.

Inscription: Lest We Forget the Lives Lost, September 11, 2001. And to Our Troops Defending Our Pride and Freedom.

Lebanon Township, New Jersey

Lebanon Township, New Jersey

The Lebanon Township 9/11 Memorial is located in Lebanon Township Memorial Park at 67 Bunnvale Road. The memorial consists of a two-story segment of steel from the World Trade Center and another piece of steel with a dedication plaque on it and a bas-relief brass rendering of the WTC as it looked prior to the attack. The plaza also has a number of benches, landscaping, and a flagpole. There is also an interesting Veterans of Foreign Wars memorial just behind this one.

Inscription: At the rising of the sun and its going down, we remember them. At the blowing of the wind and in the chill of winter, we remember them. In the opening of the buds and in the rebirth of the spring, we remember them. At the blueness of the skies and in the warmth of summer, we remember them. At the rustling of the leaves and the beauty of the autumn, we remember them. As long as we live, they too will live; for they are now a part of us. As we remember them.

Leonia, New Jersey

Leonia, New Jersey

The Bergen County World Trade Center Memorial is located in the Henry Hoebel Area of Overpeck County Park. The two granite towers are inscribed with the names of the Bergen County residents who were lost in the tragedy on September 11, 2001. The monument is surrounded by a rising wall and a pathway in the shape of a remembrance lapel ribbon, a theme which was followed by a couple of other memorials. The plaza is enclosed by landscaping and includes benches and a flagpole. It was designed by Alan Koening.

Liberty Corner, New Jersey

Liberty Corner, New Jersey

The Liberty Corner Fire Company 9/11 Memorial is located in the Liberty Corner section of Bernards Township, New Jersey. It consists of a set of stairs representing the World Trade Center stairways on which a beam from the WTC is placed. Some firefighter radio conversations appear on small plaques on each of the steps. There are also 343 memorial bricks around the memorial. **Dedicated**: September 11, 2011

Inscription: Dedicated to the honor of the 343 members of the FDNY who made the supreme sacrifice while protecting life and property in the terrorist attack upon the World Trade Center on September 11, 2001.

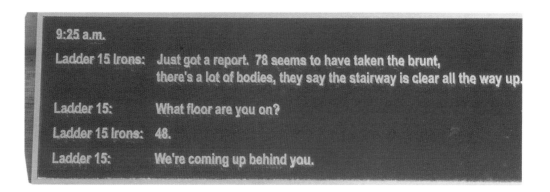

Liberty State Park, Jersey City, New Jersey

Liberty State Park, Jersey City, New Jersey

Empty Sky: the New Jersey September 11 Memorial sits in Liberty State Park in Jersey City right across the Hudson River from where the World Trade Center once stood. The memorial represents the Twin Towers lying on their sides and its brushed stainless steel walls are inscribed with the names of New Jersey's 746 residents killed on that day. Its size and design is powerful to experience.

A rusty pile of steel beams from the World Trade Center resides in front of the entrance to the walls. There is also an old train station on this site that is worth checking out as well as the Liberty Science Center, and the Statue of Liberty.

Dedicated: September 10, 2011

Liberty State Park, Jersey City, New Jersey

Inscription: On the morning of September 11, 2001, with the skies so clear that the Twin Towers across the river appeared to be within reach, the very essence of what our country stands for – freedom, tolerance, and the pursuit of happiness – was attacked. This memorial is dedicated to New Jersey's innocent loved ones who were violently and senselessly murdered that day at the World Trade Center, The Pentagon, and in Shanksville, PA.

Let this memorial reflect the legacies of those whose lives were lost, that their unfulfilled dreams and hopes may result in a better future for society. Their unique qualities and characteristics enriched our lives immeasurably and through this memorial their stories shall live on

Linden, New Jersey

The Wanda A. Green Memorial Park is located in a working-class neighborhood at 850 Mack Place. It consists of a heart-shaped plaza (unique among 9/11 memorials) with six separate monuments that are chock-full of dedicatory sentiments. The landscaped memorial also includes three flagpoles which were flying one flag when we were there.

Inscriptions: A Time to Honor, A Time to Remember, In Honor of United Airlines Flight 93 Crew and Passengers, September 11, 2001, Wanda A. Green Memorial Park *

Standing for what you believe in, regardless of the odds against you, and the pressure that tears at your resistance, means COURAGE. keeping a smile on your face when inside you feel like dying, for the sake of supporting others, means STRENGTH. *

Linden, New Jersey

Helping a friend in need, no matter the time or effort, to the best of your ability, ...means LOYALTY. Giving more than you have, and expecting nothing, but nothing in return, ...means SELFLESSNESS.*

Stopping at nothing, and doing what in your heart, you know is right, ...means DETERMINATION. Doing more than is expected, to make another's life a little more bearable without uttering a single complaint, means COMPASSION.*

Holding your head high, and being the best you know you can be, when life seems to fall apart at your feet, facing each difficulty with confidence, that time will bring you better tomorrows, and never giving up, ...means AMERICA.*

"Dedicated to the Glory of God" * John 15:13 "Greater love hath no man than this, that a man lay down his life for his friends." * United Airlines Flight 93 Crew and Passengers, On September 11, 2001, You Made The Ultimate Sacrifice To Save Others. Through Your Heroism, You Illuminated for the Entire World to See the True Path of Freedom. Your Sacrifice Will Always Be Remembered.*

Little Falls, New Jersey

The Little Falls September 11 memorial is located at Wilmore Memorial Park at Wilmore Road and Main Street. The memorial is a stone water fountain topped by two beams from the World Trade Center. The words "Never Forgotten September 11, 2001" are inscribed into the fountain's base. The park has many other memorials, including a small 9/11 plaque and tree dedicated to the first responders to the tragedy.

Manalapan, New Jersey

Manalapan, New Jersey

The Manalapan September 11 memorial is located on Route 522 in Memorial Park at the Manalapan municipal center. It consists of a pentagonal fountain, a Twin Towers replica, a couple of large memorial stones, and benches in a bricked plaza surrounded by landscaping and memorial trees.

Inscription: In Remembrance of Our Loved Ones And All Others Lost at the World Trade Center * Dedicated to the People of the United States of America in Remembrance of Their Goodness and Patriotism, 9/11 Families * Dedicated to the people of Manalapan Township in Gratitude for Their Support, Kindness and Love, 9/11 Families * For All Those Who Serve This Country in the Cause of Liberty and Freedom. In Memory of Those Who Died at The Pentagon and in Honor of Those Who Survived.

Special Info: The memorial was conceived by the students of Manalapan Englishtown Middle School.

Marlboro, New Jersey

Marlboro, New Jersey

The Marlboro September 11 memorial is located at the Marlboro municipal center.

Inscriptions: In Remembrance of All Those Who Lost Their Lives in the Tragic Events of September 11, 2001 * This Steel Beam Was Recovered from Ground Zero at the World Trade Center Site and Was Donated to the Township of Marlboro by the Sons and Daughters of America * In Everlasting Memory of the 2,976 Fallen Men and Women Who Died in New York, Washington D.C. and Pennsylvania on September 11, 2001 * In Everlasting Memory of the 40 Fallen Men and Women Who Died on United Airlines Flight #93 on September 11, 2001 * In Everlasting Memory of the 59 Fallen Men and Women Who Died on American Airlines Flight #77 and the 125 Total Men and Women Who Died in Washington D.C. on September 11, 2001 * In Everlasting Memory of the 60 Fallen Men and Women who Died on United Airlines Flight #175 and the 2,605 Total Men and Women Who Died in New York City, NY on September 11, 2001 * In Everlasting Memory of the 87 Fallen Men and Women who Died on American Airlines Flight #11 and the 2,605 Total Men and Women Who Died in New York City, NY on September 11, 2001 * In Memory of the Marlboro Residents Who Tragically Lost Their Lives on September 11, 2001

Matawan, New Jersey

There are a number of religious 9/11 memorials and this memorial at the St. Clements Roman Catholic Church is one of them. The red granite monument is tastefully understated, not too big, not too small, displaying a cross, pictures of the World Trade Center buildings, six names, and the date. The patio-sized plaza includes some benches and landscaping.

Metuchen, New Jersey

Metuchen, New Jersey

Freedom Plaza, the Metuchen 9/11 memorial sits on Main Street, at the entrance to the train station. It has a plaza, a clock tower, and a wall with the names of 700 New Jersey residents who perished in the tragedy.

Inscription (portions): Although worldwide in scope, it was a very personal tragedy for our state and our community. Mothers and fathers, sons and daughters, brothers and sisters left their families and loved ones on that fateful Tuesday morning, never to come back home. Hundreds of emergency workers went selflessly into the burning buildings, never to return.

Freedom Plaza is dedicated to those we lost on that day. May they rest in blessed memory.

In this our western world, Be Freedom's flag unfurl'd, Through all its shores! May no destructive blast, Our heaven of joy o'ercast, May Freedom's fabric last, While time endures. – *Philip Freneau, 1795*

Middlesex, New Jersey

Middlesex, New Jersey

The Middlesex Borough September 11 memorial is located at Victor Crowell Park at the intersection of Raritan Ave. and Union Ave. (Route 28). The memorial consists of an obelisk-like monument with stars and stripes represented as well as the Twin Towers as two of the monument's stripes. Another granite monument has the symbolism of the memorial explained and a September 11 timeline etched into it. There are also memorial benches and multi-colored bricks used as pavers in the plaza. The memorial is 9'11" tall and is designed by Blaise Batko who designed a number of other New Jersey memorials.

Dedicated: October 23, 2004

Inscription: In memory of Thomas F. Gorman, those in uniformed service, and all innocent civilians who lost their lives September 11, 2001

In memory of the crew and passengers of Flight 11, Flight 175, Flight 77, Flight 93

Middletown, New Jersey

Middletown, New Jersey

Middletown's World Trade Center Memorial Gardens is an emotionally powerful tribute to the 37 residents of Middletown who perished on September 11, 2001. A memorial arch marks the beginning of this thoughtful and well-designed space. The individual monuments that line the serene park-like brick path display the victims' laser-etched likenesses, names, and sentiments. Middletown lost a larger number of residents in the 9/11 tragedy than most towns due to its sizable NYC commuting population. The Memorial Gardens is located next to Middletown's train station.

Dedicated: September 11, 2003

Inscription: Dedicated to the 37 Middletown residents who lost their lives in the World Trade Center on September 11, 2001.

Monroe, New Jersey

Monroe, New Jersey

The Monroe September 11 memorial is located in the Monroe Township Memorial Park on Prospect Plains Road. The memorial consists of a Pentagon-shaped plaza bisected by a shadow-like Twin Towers in the walkway and lined by a "skyline" of nine black granite monuments which are inscribed with names of victims who perished that day. There are two flagpoles, various plaques, and some commemorative benches, all set in a beautiful walking park.

Dedicated: September 14, 2002

Inscription: In remembrance of those who were lost on September 11, 2001

In memory of all innocent civilians who lost their lives September 11, 2001

In memory of those in uniformed service who lost their lives September 11, 2001

Special Info: Designed by Blaise Batko.

Morris Plains, New Jersey

Morris Plains, New Jersey

The Morris Plains 9/11 Memorial is on Route 202 near the train station in Morris Plains. The words "Never Forget" are inscribed into the bricks of the plaza.

Inscriptions: The Morris Plains 9/11 Memorial is dedicated to each of the individuals who perished in the worst attack on American soil in our history. May we never forget the 2,984 victims who lost their lives at the World Trade Center, The Pentagon, and in Shanksville, Pennsylvania. The Memorial includes three interconnected steel columns from the North Tower of the WTC that measure 23 feet in height. The steel is set on a pentagon-shaped base that is surrounded by a circle symbolic of the continuity of life. The grassy terrain on either side of the flagpoles and two red maple trees are in remembrance of those on Flight 93 who valiantly prevented further horror on a field in Shanksville, PA.

While thousands were rushing out of the World Trade Center, hundreds of brave firefighters, police and other public safety personnel were bravely and unselfishly rushing in. We remember the 442 first responders—including 343 NYC Firefighters, 38 Port Authority Police Officers, and 27 NYC Police Officers—who made the ultimate sacrifice in order to help thousands of civilians working at the WTC safely escape the attacks.

Mountainside, New Jersey

Mountainside, New Jersey

The Union County September 11 Memorial is located at Echo Lake County Park at Mill Road and Park Drive in Mountainside. This beautiful memorial has as its focus two steel beams from the World Trade Center site set in a Pentagon-shaped area of the brick-paved plaza. Another area of focus of this memorial is the sculpted hand holding an eternal flame very similar to the Statue of Liberty's torch celebrating Freedom. Also included in this memorial is a remembrance ribbon shape made of walkway pavers, a memorial plaque affixed to a concrete pedestal, three flagpoles, and a number of benches all surrounded by a professionally landscaped park.

Inscription: The County of Union dedicates this memorial to the residents of Union County, their families, and all other individuals who lost their lives in the attacks of September 11, 2001. You are in our hearts forever.

Mount Laurel, New Jersey

Mount Laurel, New Jersey

In Memorium is a privately sponsored September 11 metal sculpture in an office park owned by the large real estate investment trust Liberty Property Trust. It is located in the Greentree North Corporate Center on Commerce Parkway.

Inscription: In Memorium of those who lived and died, suffered and fought to save lives for America and its people due to the tragic events of 9-11-01. Liberty Property Trust

New Providence, New Jersey

New Providence, New Jersey

The New Providence September 11 Memorial is located in Centennial Park outside the library and across from the police station. The memorial consists of a large, contorted piece of steel from the World Trade Center and a tile painting from Flower Mound, Texas with 9/11 imagery and sentiments. There is also a 9/11 time capsule buried in this same park a few feet away.

Inscription: We will remember…. To the people of New Providence, from the people of Flower Mound, Texas, we offer this memorial as our solemn pledge to remember you. Because of September 11, 2001, we unite in brotherhood to share your grief, offer strength in community and embrace hope for America's future.

Newton, New Jersey

Newton, New Jersey

The Sussex County 9-11 Monument is located on the campus of Sussex County Community College.

Inscriptions: September 11, 2001 We Will Never Forget * Flight 175 * Flight 93 * Flight 77 * Flight 11

Sussex County 9-11 Monument. On September 11, 2001 four U.S. planes were hijacked by terrorists. Two planes were crashed into the Twin Towers of the World Trade Center in New York City, one into the Pentagon and one into a field in Pennsylvania. In total, more than 3,000 people; Civilians, Police-Officers, Firefighters and Military personnel were killed in a matter of a few hours. The national tragedy affected numerous Sussex County residents who were related to or knew a victim of the attack on America as well as the many residents of Sussex County who worked in the rescue, recovery and relief efforts afterward. This Monument was constructed by the citizens of Sussex County as an everlasting tribute to the memories of those who lost their lives, to serve as a symbol honoring the heroic service and sacrifices unselfishly made on that tragic day and to help us to Never Forget the charity of the thousands of Americans who rushed to the aid of the fallen during the hours, days, and months following the attack. Standing a total of 9 feet 11 inches tall, the Monument's centerpiece is an actual steel beam recovered from the World Trade Center – Ground Zero by Port Authority Police Officers and brought back here by the Sussex County Policemen's Benevolent Association, Local No. 138. The beam is featured rising up out of rubble-like granite, signifying the steel of American resolve.

North Arlington, New Jersey

North Arlington, New Jersey

The Archdiocese of Newark's Catholic Cemeteries 9/11 Memorial is located at Holy Cross Cemetery on 340 Ridge Road. It is the largest cemetery that we have ever been in, so the place is already impressive. The memorial is not easy to find within the cemetery and I suggest driving into the cemetery to find it, not walking as we initially did. It is a very impressive memorial and is located near some 9/11 grave sites as well. The memorial remembers the innocent victims of the tragedy as well as the selfless first responders. The twenty foot towers have an open area which echoes the impacts to the Twin Towers. A cross hangs within the towers to remind viewers that God was present during the tragedy. The site includes polished granite benches, three inspirational quotes from the Bible etched in polished granite stones, images of the tragedy permanently affixed to the memorial, a flagpole, and some steel from the WTC.

Inscriptions: Do not be conquered by evil, but conquer evil with good. – Romans 12:21

I am the resurrection and the life, whoever believes in me, even though they die, will live. John 11:25-26

Nothing will be able to separate us from the love of God in Christ Jesus our Lord. Romans 8:39

North Brunswick, New Jersey

North Brunswick, New Jersey

As shown on the previous page, the North Brunswick 9/11 memorial also has two marble tablets with the names of every victim who perished , along with its central monument of granite hands holding up steel from the WTC.

Inscription: September 11, 2001 was a day of loss, bravery, and togetherness for our nation. On that day, two hijacked airplanes crashed into the World Trade Center towers in New York City, one hijacked plane crashed into the Pentagon in Washington, DC, and a fourth hijacked plane crashed in a Pennsylvania field due to the courage and strength of the self-sacrificing passengers on board. Even in our darkest hour, the courage and hope of many Americans were shining bright as we mourned our losses, picked up the pieces, and dedicated ourselves to our communities and country. The North Brunswick September 11 committee was formed to commemorate the individuals we lost and to forever honor their memories. The North Brunswick September 11th memorial, featuring granite hands holding twisted pieces of steel from the World Trade Centers, reflects our belief that our community will not forget the events of that fateful day and will always hold close the memories of the 2,973 lives lost. | 343 firefighters lost | 23 NYPD police officers lost | 37 Port Authority police officers lost | 7 EMS workers lost

Old Bridge, New Jersey

Old Bridge, New Jersey

The Old Bridge September 11 memorial is a circular plaza ringed with hedges, trees, and twelve square granite blocks representing the residents who died from Old Bridge. A flag flies at the top of the circle behind the monument. Three plaques, one with a timeline of the terrible event, one with donor and committee member names, and one plaque which lies in front of the polished granite Twin Towers monument and expresses a dedication statement within a city skyline. The memorial is located on township property in front of the library.

Dedicated: September 11, 2002

Inscription: The morning of September 11, 2001 will forever be etched in our hearts and minds. The tragic and horrific attack on our country took the lives of many innocent loved ones. This memorial is dedicated to the twelve Old Bridge residents and all those who lost their lives on that day. May their legacy be to inspire us to work together as a community toward a better future.

Special Info: Designed by Blaise Batko.

Old Bridge, New Jersey – Cheesequake Fire Department Memorial

Parsippany, New Jersey

Parsippany, New Jersey

The Morris County September 11, 2001 Memorial is on West Hanover Avenue in Parsippany.

Inscription: This memorial is dedicated to every victim of the September 11, 2001 attacks against our country. May we never forget those who lost their lives at the World Trade Center, the Pentagon, on United Airlines Flight #93 and #175, and American Airlines Flight #11 and #77. May they be forever remembered along with the police, fire, emergency services personnel and civilian heroes who gave their lives on this tragic day. May the families and loved ones of the victims, and all visitors to this memorial, find solace in this tribute to those who perished.

This memorial is comprised of 3 steel sections from the World Trade Center, pieces of United Flight #93, and soil from the Pentagon. The concrete blocks at the base of the steel represent the foundations of our lives: family, relationships and community. The recurring circular forms signify the continuance of life. The water surrounding the memorial symbolizes healing and rebirth. The island on which the steel beams stand and the connecting bridges suggest the blending of ethnic, cultural and spiritual differences. Finally, the flowers between the concrete blocks represent life and hope, reminding us that with the passing of time comes healing, peace and resolve.

Pennsauken, New Jersey

Pennsauken, New Jersey

The Camden County Victims of Terrorism Memorial is located in Cooper River Park in Pennsauken. It consists of seven interconnected pillars, each with a plaque descriptive of a terrorist event against the United States, including September 11, 2001. Camden County's victims are also listed on the plaques. There is also a bench and a tree planted in the center of the structure. The memorial's designer is John Giannotti. The events memorialized are shown here:

April 18, 1983 – U.S. Embassy in Beirut	October 23, 1983 – U.S. Marine barracks in Beirut	December 21, 1988 – Pan Am 103 over Lockerbie, Scotland	February 26, 1993 – World Trade Center in New York	April 19, 1995 – The Alfred P. Murrah Federal Building, Oklahoma City	August 7 1998 – U.S. embassies in Kenya and Tanzania	October 12, 2000 – U.S.S. Cole while docked in the Gulf of Yemen	September 11, 2001 – World Trade Center, Pentagon, Shanksville, Pennsylvania

Pennsauken, New Jersey

Pennsauken, New Jersey

The Pennsauken 9/11 memorial is located on Route 130 at Merchantville Avenue. It was designed by Brian P. Hanlon who also created Brick's 9/11 monument. Three large pieces vie for the viewer's attention in this memorial. A bronze sculpture on a pentagonal base surrounded by pentagonal paved area with memorial pavers, a granite wall representing New York City's skyline with the title of the memorial and a timeline of the day's events, and a large steel beam from the WTC. All of this is in a meticulously landscaped park including three flagpoles. The tribute was dedicated on September 11, 2003.

Inscriptions: "We Shall Never Forget" September 11, 2001

Peace * Compassion * Bravery * Courage * Hope

Steel recovered from the World Trade Center after September 11, 2001 courtesy of The Port Authority of NY & NJ and is displayed in memory of 2,752 victims including: 343 New York City Firefighters, 37 Port Authority Police Officers, 23 New York City Police Officers

Saddle River, New Jersey

The Saddle River 9/11 Memorial is on East Allendale Road in Saddle River. The memorial consists of a globe-topped fountain, a memorial plaque honoring the town's three victims, a circular walkway and a bench in a small, landscaped park.

Inscription: September 11, 2001 Remembered * Though nothing can bring back the hour of splendour in the grass, of glory in the flower, we will grieve not, rather find strength in what remains behind – William Wordsworth * In honour of the lives of these three good men, our dear friends and neighbors, we will forever defy tyranny so that we may live with everlasting freedom. God Bless America

Sayreville, New Jersey

Sayreville, New Jersey

Sayreville's September 11 memorial is located at Burkes Park on Washington Road. The memorial is a circular brick plaza including steel from the World Trade Center, a replica of the Twin Towers, granite benches with inscriptions, and 3 flagpoles with more inscriptions at the base of one of them (mention is made of the Pentagon, Shanksville, and World Trade Center heroes).

Inscription: In Honor and Memory of Our Loved Ones and All Others Lost on "9-11-2001"

The benches have inscriptions like "Gone but not forgotten", and "Heroes of 9-11 Lost", and "God Bless America - In the spirit of Freedom and Democracy".

Seaside Heights, New Jersey

The Borough of Seaside Heights September 11 memorial is located at 901 Boulevard next to the police station. It consists of a clock sitting in a pentagon-shaped brick and concrete base with seats, planters, and memorial plaques.

Inscription: "Take Time to Remember" Through the donations of a caring community, this clock has been erected in remembrance of the September 11, 2001 attacks on the American nation by cowardly terrorists. It is a tribute to honor the innocent lives that were lost that day. Taking time to remember their sacrifice affirms love and appreciation of the principals of freedom and opportunity for which the United States of America so proudly stands.

Secaucus, New Jersey

Secaucus, New Jersey

The Secaucus 9/11 memorial is located in front of the library at 1379 Paterson Plank Road.

Inscription: On September 11, 2001, the nation was stunned by horrific acts of terrorism never before experienced on American soil. A handful of cowardly terrorists used commercial airliners to destroy the Twin Towers of the World Trade Center in New York City and damage the Pentagon in Washington D.C., causing thousands of innocent people to lose their lives. Nowhere was this devastation felt more keenly than in the town of Secaucus which lost six of its own family of residents. These acts of terrorism broke the hearts and tried the souls of us all, but they did not break our spirit. In their names, and in the names of countless others who left unfillable spaces in family circles, we resolve to remember them always and do good deeds in their memory. Our lives will be forever changed by these cowardly attacks on our nation and our community, but we will move forward – together, united, and stronger than ever. "Freedom and fear are at war. The advance of human freedom, the great achievement of our time, and the great hope of every time, now depends on us. Our nation, this generation, will lift a dark threat of violence from our people and our future. We will rally the world to this cause by our efforts, by our courage. We will not tire, we will not falter, and we will not fail." – George W. Bush President of the United States of America * "We look with sorrow at the loss of thousands of lives from the criminal atrocities that have occurred in New York and Washington, and we feel the pain in our hearts and right here in our own community." – Dennis Elwell Mayor of Secaucus.

Somerset, New Jersey

The Somerset Fire and Rescue 9/11 memorial consists of a plaque, and a steel beam from the World Trade Center and two flagpoles on a small patio in the parking lot of the Somerset Fire and Rescue station at 14 Hollywood Avenue. Somerset is a section of Franklin Township.

Dedicated: September 11, 2011

Inscription: September 11, 2001 We Shall Never Forget

Somerville, New Jersey

Somerville, New Jersey

The Somerset County 9/11 Memorial is located on East Main Street in Somerville near the Somerset County Courthouse. The memorial consists of a clock tower, a beam from the WTC, a plaque with the names of the victims, and a fire alarm box, all set in a circular plaza with benches. **Dedicated**: 2004

Inscription: (beam) The citizens of Somerset County dedicate this memorial to the thousands of innocent lives lost on September 11, 2001 and to the families that loved them. From this county we remember and honor: (39 Somerset residents named on the plaque are mentioned in the appendix of this book). (clock) A Time to Remember (alarm box) This alarm box is dedicated in memory of the 343 NY firefighters who answered their final alarm on September 11, 2001

South Amboy, New Jersey

South Amboy, New Jersey

The Middlesex County Victims of Terrorism Memorial is located on the waterfront at Raritan Bay Park in South Amboy. The tile-paved plaza includes seating, a pillared gazebo, and a stately bronze eagle statue mounted on a pentagonal marble base. The eagle's eyes gaze out across the water to where the World Trade Center once stood.

Dedicated: 2003

Inscription: May our country itself become a vast and splendid monument, not of oppression and terror, but of wisdom, of peace, and of liberty, upon which the world may gaze with admiration forever. – *Daniel Webster*

Special Info: The memorial is based on the designs of three Middlesex County high school students who had submitted concepts to a county-wide design competition.

South River, New Jersey

South River, New Jersey

The South River 9/11 memorial is located at Dailey's Pond park. It consists of the central monument of a skyline with an ethereal Twin Towers rising above it, a plaza, inscribed granite benches, a flagpole, and a brick-lined path with individual inscribed donors and memorial sentiments on each brick.

Dedicated: September 11, 2003

Inscription: In memory of Christopher More Dincuff and all innocent civilians who lost their lives September 11, 2001

In memory of those in uniformed service who lost their lives September 11, 2001

Special Info: Designed by Blaise Batko.

Spotswood, New Jersey

The Spotswood 9/11 memorial resides near the Spotswood High School and municipal complex. It incorporates a granite Twin Towers facsimile with steel from the World Trade Center on a pentagonal granite base surrounded by a pentagon-shaped walkway. There is also a bench, flagpole, and "trees grown from trees from the grounds of the WTC."

Dedicated: September 11, 2005

Inscription: Spotswood honors the victims and heroes of September 11, 2001

Special Info: The memorial is based on the design of the Spotswood High School History Club.

Stirling, New Jersey

Stirling, New Jersey

The Tower of Remembrance September 11 memorial at the Shrine of St. Joseph is at 1050 Long Hill Road in Stirling. The memorial contains large steel beams from the North Tower of the WTC and bells from a seminary in Virginia. The names of all the victims are inscribed on plaques on the memorial walls. The bells toll at 46 minutes after each hour (until 8:46 pm) and ring four times in remembrance of those who died in each of the Twin Towers, the Pentagon, and in Pennsylvania.

Inscription: September 11, 2001 "We Will Remember"

Toms River, New Jersey

The Toms River September 11 memorial is located next to the Ocean County Library at 101 Washington Street. It is a simple inscribed polished granite stone.

Inscription: This memorial is placed in memory of the innocent people, heroic firemen, policemen and rescue workers who died during the attack on the Twin Towers, the Pentagon and on the airliners used as tools of destruction. * OUR BRIGHTEST DAY They want us to remember tons of dust and twisted steel. They think they can destroy us, that we will never heal. They want our world to crumble and say that it's "God's plan". But it's God's love that unites us, each and every man. Their evil has attacked us all and filled our hearts with fear. So now we must recover and grow stronger with each tear. We must pray to God for guidance, to show us all the way. Our faith will turn this time of darkness into our brightest day! – Samantha L. Ruocco 8th Grade Student Toms River Schools * United We Stand Dedicated on behalf of the people of Dover Township 9-11-2002

Toms River, New Jersey

The Ocean County September 11 memorial is located in Toms River across from the Ocean County Court on Hooper Avenue. The memorial consists of an inscribed and laser-etched, polished granite stone monument and a smaller monument with a piece of WTC steel attached to it.

Inscriptions: America was targeted for attack because we're the brightest beacon for freedom and opportunity in the world. And no one will keep that light from shining. – President George W. Bush September 11, 2001

* In memory of September 11, 2001 for all those lives lost. For all those lives touched. Our lives – forever changed. 3047 people lost their lives 19 were residents of Ocean County. * World Trade Center steel presented to the citizens of Ocean County on the tenth anniversary of the attacks of Sept. 11, 2001. With a heavy heart, America will remember forever.

Union Beach, New Jersey

Union Beach, New Jersey

The Union Beach September 11 memorial is a laser-etched polished granite or marble monument with a photo-realistic image of the NYC skyline and an inscription on a Twin Towers-shaped block of stone. It's located on the beach looking across the Raritan Bay to the spot where the World Trade Center once stood.

Dedicated: June 29, 2002

Inscription: See photo on previous page.

Union City, New Jersey

The Union City September 11 memorial is just across 30th Street from the post office on Palisade Avenue. It is a small affair with a monument, a piece of steel from the WTC, and a plaque. The brick-paved plaza also has some benches, a flagpole, and some landscaping.

Inscription: September 11, 2001   May we never forget the thousands of human beings who perished in the destruction of the World Trade Center New York City. The spectacular vision which was once the World Trade Center towers is now vanished from our view but will remain in our memory forever. We will stand vigilant against those who wish to harm the United States of America and her people "...one nation, under God, indivisible with Liberty and Justice for all..."

Verona, New Jersey

Verona, New Jersey

The Verona September 11 Memorial is located at 600 Bloomfield Avenue at the Verona municipal center.

Inscriptions: "Today our way of life, our very freedom came under attack in a series of deliberate and deadly terrorist acts. These acts shattered steel but they cannot dent the steel of American resolve." – President George W. Bush Address to the Nation September 11, 2001 *

Dedicated to all victims and heroes of the September 11, 2001 attacks in New York City, Shanksville PA, Washington, D.C. *

In remembrance of (2) Verona residents who perished in the attack and collapse of The Twin Towers World Trade Center New York City *

Salvaged steel from the Twin Towers. Let it remind us that America's freedom must never be taken for granted.

Westfield, New Jersey

Westfield, New Jersey

The Westfield September 11th Memorial Park is on North Avenue West and East Broad Street. The names of all 9/11 victims are inscribed on the blue glass of the obelisk/monument. There are twelve smaller granite obelisks here, each one with the name of a Westfield victim. The park is beautifully landscaped and accompanied by a flagpole. It looks great at night as each small obelisk is lit as well as the main obelisk being lit by a few spotlights which give it a cool blue glow.

Dedicated: September 21, 2002

Inscription: In Memory of Those Who Perished * Hope * Peace * Renewal

West New York, New Jersey

West New York, New Jersey

The West New York September 11 Memorial is located in Donnelly Park on Kennedy Boulevard East and Hillside Road. It boasts an impressive view of the New York City skyline which is worth seeing by itself. The memorial consists of a sculpture of a blindfolded Lady Justice holding the scales of justice while standing atop a pedestal. In the warm months the water is turned on in the fountain below her. The memorial includes a roughly circular plaza bordered by benches and landscaping. Three flagpoles stand on the river side of the memorial. Dedicated September 11, 2002.

Inscriptions: Lady Justice and fountain dedicated to the victims and heroes of the attack on America, September 11, 2001

"In honor of the victims and heroes, both praised and unsung. May they dwell in the house and heart of history." – Janet Lewis, West New York

West Orange, New Jersey

West Orange, New Jersey

The Essex County September 11 Memorial is at Eagle Rock Reservation overlooking the New York City skyline. This beautiful and emotion-charged memorial was dedicated on October 20, 2002. The memorial consists of many different monuments to those lost including a bronze bald eagle with an eight-foot wing span, a book with the names of those lost from Essex County, and a girl with a teddy bear. On either side are a fireman's helmet and a police officer's hat. To the left is a teenage boy holding a lantern and gazing toward the skyline. The former barrier wall was replaced by polished granite with the names and home towns of all who were lost in the attacks. There are also seven dogwood trees along a side path for each of the four hijacked planes, the Pentagon, and the two World Trade Center Towers. Designed and built by Cedar Grove sculptor and artist Patrick Morelli.

Inscription: "Remembrance and Rebirth" *

West Orange, New Jersey

Inscriptions: With deepest gratitude from the people of Essex County, New Jersey, in memory of the 23 New York City Police Officers, 37 Port Authority of New York and New Jersey Police Officers and Emergency Medical Services Personnel who sacrificed their lives in the line of duty on September 11, 2001. *

With deepest gratitude from the people of Essex County, New Jersey, in memory of the 343 New York City Firefighters who sacrificed their lives in the line of duty on September 11, 2001. *

For the Children Who Lost Loved Ones "Gabriella" *

In Memory of the Flight Crew Members Who Sacrificed Their Lives in the Line Of Duty on September 11, 2001 *

This tree is dedicated in loving memory of the casualties of the September 11, 2001 attack on our nation who lost their lives on *American Airlines Flight 11*--each one a patriot and hero forever. May the world always reflect on their bravery and never forget their sacrifice for our freedom. May those of us left behind find comfort from our sorrow. * [This same sentiment is also inscribed on plaques in front of trees dedicated to United Flights 93 and 175, American Airlines Flight 77, One World Trade Center, Two World Trade Center, and The Pentagon.]

September 11, 2001 A Day When People Responded to Terror with Full Hearts and Helping Hands. Emergency Medical Service personnel across the country were among the first responders to all sites under attack. While NY Fire Department EMTs sped to the shattered World Trade Center, EMTs on this side of the Hudson River began to treat and comfort survivors arriving by ferry at Hoboken and Jersey City. Several EMTs were among those trapped and lost as the Twin Towers collapsed – and many others remained to labor for months, joined by volunteers from all over America, to clear rubble and search for remains. These brave men and women have earned the respect and recognition of our grateful nation. Dedicated this 11th day of September, 2011. *

September 11, 2001 A Day We Will Always Remember. This piece of steel and concrete is from the foundation of the Twin Towers, first bombed in 1993 and attacked and destroyed in 2001. It rests here as a reminder that America, full of freedom and possibilities, will survive and flourish and that the people who were directly impacted by this heart-breaking tragedy will forever remain in our hearts and minds. Dedicated this 11th day of September 2011 *

West Windsor, New Jersey

West Windsor, New Jersey

The Mercer County September 11 Memorial is located near the Marina at Mercer County Park.

Inscriptions: "There are two ways of exerting one's strength: one is pushing down, the other is pulling up." *–Booker T. Washington*

THE EVENT On September 11, 2001, America suffered an assault on its home soil that resulted in almost 3000 dead and countless others physically and emotionally wounded. The victims were nationals of more than 70 countries, making this tragedy global in impact. Dedicated on this, the 11th day of September, 2011 on the 10th Anniversary of September 11, this memorial is a lasting tribute to the heroes who perished. Lest we forget.

THE SCULPTURE The Twin Towers of the World Trade Center in New York City are an icon of the events of September 11, 2001, and a constant reminder of the human loss there, at the Pentagon in Washington D.C. and in Shanksville, Pennsylvania. This monument displays a segment of a steel girder salvaged from the World Trade Center site in the aftermath of the attack. The steel cable was part of a World Trade Center elevator and was acquired only a few months before tragedy struck. They are displayed here in a simple setting to keep fresh in our memories the stark reality of September 11th and to encourage reflection on the events of that day and their enduring consequences.

Westwood, New Jersey

The Westwood September 11 memorial is located on Broadway and Westwood Avenue in a park near the train station. The memorial consists of a plaza with some granite memorial stones and a red, white, and blue brick walkway in the shape of a remembrance ribbon. The center of the memorial is the brick planter in which sits an unruly Japanese maple. The planter is bounded on four sides by memorial stones in tribute to Westwood's lost residents. The walkway wraps around the memorial and is lined by granite benches.

Woodbridge, New Jersey

The Woodbridge September 11 memorial consists of a laser-etched marble or granite monument with a photo-realistic image of U.S. flag, and an angel watching over three uniformed rescue workers, and the New York City skyline including the World Trade Center. The monument, which also includes the names of Woodbridge residents lost that day, is located at the municipal center on Main Street.

Inscription: Woodbridge remembers those whose spirit shines in the darkness. 9-11-01

The Victims of September 11, 2001

World Trade Center Victims

Gordon M. Aamoth, Jr.
Edelmiro Abad
Maria Rose Abad
Andrew Anthony Abate
Vincent Abate
Laurence Christopher Abel
William F. Abrahamson
Richard Anthony Aceto
Jesus Acevedo Rescand
Heinrich Bernhard Ackermann
Paul Acquaviva
Donald LaRoy Adams
Patrick Adams
Shannon Lewis Adams
Stephen George Adams
Ignatius Udo Adanga
Christy A. Addamo
Terence E. Adderley, Jr.
Sophia Buruwad Addo
Lee Allan Adler
Daniel Thomas Afflitto
Emmanuel Akwasi Afuakwah
Alok Agarwal
Mukul Kumar Agarwala
Joseph Agnello
David Scott Agnes
Brian G. Ahearn
Jeremiah Joseph Ahern
Joanne Marie Ahladiotis
Shabbir Ahmed
Terrance Andre Aiken
Godwin Ajala
Gertrude M. Alagero
Andrew Alameno
Margaret Ann Alario
Gary M. Albero
Jon Leslie Albert
Peter Alderman
Jacquelyn Delaine Aldridge
David D. Alger
Sarah Ali-Escarcega
Ernest Alikakos
Edward L. Allegretto
Eric Allen
Joseph Ryan Allen
Richard Dennis Allen
Richard Lanard Allen
Christopher E. Allingham
Janet M. Alonso
Arturo Alva-Moreno
Anthony Alvarado
Antonio Javier Alvarez
Victoria Alvarez-Brito
Telmo E. Alvear
Cesar Amoranto Alviar
Tariq Amanullah
Angelo Amaranto

James M. Amato Joseph Amatuccio
Christopher Charles Amoroso
Kazuhiro Anai
Calixto Anaya, Jr.
Joseph Anchundia
Kermit Charles Anderson
Yvette Constance Anderson
John Andreacchio
Michael Rourke Andrews
Jean Ann Andrucki
Siew-Nya Ang
Joseph Angelini, Jr.
Joseph Angelini, Sr.
Laura Angilletta
Doreen J. Angrisani
Lorraine Antigua
Peter Paul Apollo
Faustino Apostol, Jr.
Frank Thomas Aquilino
Patrick Michael Aranyos
David Arce
Michael George Arczynski
Louis Arena
Adam P. Arias
Michael Armstrong
Jack Charles Aron
Joshua Aron
Richard Avery Aronow
Japhet Jesse Aryee
Patrick Asante
Carl Asaro
Michael Asciak
Michael Edward Asher
Janice Marie Ashley
Thomas J. Ashton
Manuel O. Asitimbay
Gregg Arthur Atlas
Gerald T. Atwood
James Audiffred
Louis Frank Aversano, Jr.
Ezra Aviles
Sandy Ayala
Arlene T. Babakitis
Eustace P. Bacchus
John J. Badagliacca
Jane Ellen Baeszler
Robert J. Baierwalter
Andrew J. Bailey
Brett T. Bailey
Tatyana Bakalinskaya
Michael S. Baksh
Sharon M. Balkcom
Michael Andrew Bane
Katherine Bantis
Gerard Baptiste
Walter Baran
Gerard A. Barbara
Paul Vincent Barbaro
James William Barbella

Ivan Kyrillos F. Barbosa
Victor Daniel Barbosa
Colleen Ann Barkow
David Michael Barkway
Matthew Barnes
Sheila Patricia Barnes
Evan J. Baron
Renee Barrett-Arjune
Nathaly Barrios La Cruz
Arthur Thaddeus Barry
Diane G. Barry
Maurice Vincent Barry
Scott D. Bart
Carlton W. Bartels
Guy Barzvi
Inna B. Basina
Alysia Basmajian
Kenneth William Basnicki
Steven Bates
Paul James Battaglia
Walter David Bauer, Jr.
Marlyn Capito Bautista
Jasper Baxter
Michele Beale
Paul Frederick Beatini
Jane S. Beatty
Lawrence Ira Beck
Manette Marie Beckles
Carl John Bedigian
Michael Earnest Beekman
Maria A. Behr
Yelena Belilovsky
Nina Patrice Bell
Debbie Bellows
Stephen Elliot Belson
Paul M. Benedetti
Denise Lenore Benedetto
Maria Bengochea
Bryan Craig Bennett
Eric L. Bennett
Oliver Duncan Bennett
Margaret L. Benson
Dominick J. Berardi
James Patrick Berger
Steven Howard Berger
John P. Bergin
Alvin Bergsohn
Daniel Bergstein
Michael J. Berkeley
Donna M. Bernaerts
David W. Bernard
William Bernstein
David M. Berray
David S. Berry
Joseph J. Berry
William Reed Bethke
Timothy Betterly
Edward Frank Beyea
Paul Beyer

Anil Tahilram Bharvaney
Bella J. Bhukhan
Shimmy D. Biegeleisen
Peter Alexander Bielfeld
William G. Biggart
Brian Bilcher
Carl Vincent Bini
Gary Eugene Bird
Joshua David Birnbaum
George John Bishop
Jeffrey Donald Bittner
Albert Balewa Blackman, Jr.
Christopher Joseph Blackwell
Susan Leigh Blair
Harry Blanding, Jr.
Janice Lee Blaney
Craig Michael Blass
Rita Blau
Richard Middleton Blood, Jr.
Michael Andrew Boccardi
John P. Bocchi
Michael Leopoldo Bocchino
Susan M. Bochino
Bruce D. Boehm
Mary Catherine Boffa
Nicholas Andrew Bogdan
Darren Christopher Bohan
Lawrence Francis Boisseau
Vincent M. Boland, Jr.
Alan Bondarenko
Andre Bonheur, Jr.
Colin Arthur Bonnett
Frank Bonomo
Yvonne Lucia Bonomo
Genieve Bonsignore, 3
Seaon Booker
Sherry Ann Bordeaux
Krystine Bordenabe
Martin Boryczewski
Richard Edward Bosco
John H. Boulton
Francisco Eligio Bourdier
Thomas Harold Bowden, Jr.
Kimberly S. Bowers
Veronique Nicole Bowers
Larry Bowman
Shawn Edward Bowman, Jr.
Kevin L. Bowser
Gary R. Box
Gennady Boyarsky
Pamela Boyce
Michael Boyle
Alfred Braca
Kevin Bracken
David Brian Brady
Alexander Braginsky
Nicholas W. Brandemarti
Michelle Renee Bratton
Patrice Braut
Lydia E. Bravo
Ronald Michael Breitweiser
Edward A. Brennan III
Francis Henry Brennan
Michael E. Brennan

Peter Brennan
Thomas M. Brennan
Daniel J. Brethel
Gary Lee Bright
Jonathan Briley
Mark A. Brisman
Paul Gary Bristow
Mark Francis Broderick
Herman Charles Broghammer
Keith A. Broomfield
Ethel Brown Janice
Juloise Brown
Lloyd Stanford Brown
Patrick J. Brown
Bettina Browne
Mark Bruce
Richard George Bruehert
Andrew Brunn
Vincent Brunton
Ronald Paul Bucca
Brandon J. Buchanan
Gregory Joseph Buck
Dennis Buckley
Nancy Clare Bueche
Patrick Joseph Buhse
John Edwards Bulaga, Jr.
Stephen Bunin
Matthew J. Burke
Thomas Daniel Burke
William Francis Burke, Jr.
Donald J. Burns
Kathleen Anne Burns
Keith James Burns
John Patrick Burnside
Irina Buslo
Milton G. Bustillo
Thomas M. Butler
Patrick Byrne
Timothy G. Byrne
Jesus Neptali Cabezas
Lillian Caceres
Brian Joseph Cachia
Steven Dennis Cafiero, Jr.
Richard M. Caggiano
Cecile Marella Caguicla
Michael John Cahill
Scott Walter Cahill
Thomas Joseph Cahill
George Cain
Salvatore B. Calabro
Joseph Calandrillo
Philip V. Calcagno
Edward Calderon
Kenneth Marcus Caldwell
Dominick Enrico Calia
Felix Calixte
Frank Callahan
Liam Callahan
Luigi Calvi
Roko Camaj
Michael F. Cammarata
David Otey Campbell
Geoffrey Thomas Campbell
Jill Marie Campbell

Robert Arthur Campbell
Sandra Patricia Campbell
Sean Thomas Canavan
John A. Candela
Vincent Cangelosi
Stephen J. Cangialosi
Lisa Bella Cannava
Brian Cannizzaro
Michael Canty
Louis Anthony Caporicci
Jonathan Neff Cappello
James Christopher Cappers
Richard Michael Caproni
Jose Manuel Cardona
Dennis M. Carey
Steve Carey
Edward Carlino
Michael Scott Carlo
David G. Carlone
Rosemarie C. Carlson
Mark Stephen Carney
Joyce Ann Carpeneto
Ivhan Luis Carpio Bautista
Jeremy M. Carrington
Michael Carroll
Peter Carroll
James Joseph Carson, Jr.
Marcia Cecil Carter
James Marcel Cartier
Vivian Casalduc
John Francis Casazza
Paul R. Cascio
Margarito Casillas
Thomas Anthony Casoria
William Otto Caspar
Alejandro Castano
Arcelia Castillo
Germaan Castillo Garcia
Leonard M. Castrianno
Jose Ramon Castro
Richard G. Catarelli
Christopher Sean Caton
Robert John Caufield
Mary Teresa Caulfield
Judson Cavalier
Michael Joseph Cawley
Jason David Cayne
Juan Armando Ceballos
Jason Michael Cefalu
Thomas Joseph Celic
Ana Mercedes Centeno
Joni Cesta
Jeffrey Marc Chairnoff
Swarna Chalasani
William Chalcoff
Eli Chalouh
Charles Lawrence Chan
Mandy Chang
Mark Lawrence Charette
Gregorio Manuel Chavez
Delrose E. Cheatham
Pedro Francisco Checo
Douglas MacMillan Cherry
Stephen Patrick Cherry

Vernon Paul Cherry
Nester Julio Chevalier
Swede Chevalier
Alexander H. Chiang
Dorothy J. Chiarchiaro
Luis Alfonso Chimbo
Robert Chin
Wing Wai Ching
Nicholas Paul Chiofalo
John Chipura
Peter A. Chirchirillo
Catherine Chirls
Kyung Hee Cho
Abul K. Chowdhury
Mohammad Salahuddin Chowdhury
Kirsten L. Christophe
Pamela Chu
Steven Chucknick
Wai Chung
Christopher Ciafardini
Alex F. Ciccone
Frances Ann Cilente
Elaine Cillo
Edna Cintron
Nestor Andre Cintron III
Robert Dominick Cirri
Juan Pablo Cisneros-Alvarez
Benjamin Keefe Clark
Eugene Clark
Gregory Alan Clark
Mannie Leroy Clark
Thomas R. Clark
Christopher Robert Clarke
Donna Marie Clarke
Michael J. Clarke
Suria Rachel Emma Clarke
Kevin Francis Cleary
James D. Cleere
Geoffrey W. Cloud
Susan Marie Clyne
Steven Coakley
Jeffrey Alan Coale
Patricia A. Cody
Daniel Michael Coffey
Jason M. Coffey
Florence G. Cohen
Kevin Sanford Cohen
Anthony Joseph Coladonato
Mark Joseph Colaio
Stephen Colaio
Christopher M. Colasanti
Kevin Nathaniel Colbert
Michel P. Colbert
Keith E. Coleman
Scott Thomas Coleman
Tarel Coleman
Liam Joseph Colhoun
Robert D. Colin
Robert J. Coll
Jean Collin
John Michael Collins
Michael L. Collins
Thomas J. Collins
Joseph Collison

Patricia Malia Colodner
Linda M. Colon
Sol E. Colon
Ronald Edward Comer
Sandra Jolane Conaty Brace
Jaime Concepcion
Albert Conde
Denease Conley
Susan P. Conlon
Margaret Mary Conner
Cynthia Marie Lise Connolly
John E. Connolly, Jr.
James Lee Connor
Jonathan M. Connors
Kevin Patrick Connors
Kevin F. Conroy
Jose Manuel Contreras-Fernandez
Brenda E. Conway
Dennis Michael Cook
Helen D. Cook
John A. Cooper
Joseph John Coppo, Jr.
Gerard J. Coppola
Joseph Albert Corbett
Alejandro Cordero
Robert Cordice
Ruben D. Correa
Danny A. Correa-Gutierrez
James J. Corrigan
Carlos Cortes
Kevin Cosgrove
Dolores Marie Costa
Digna Alexandra Costanza
Charles Gregory Costello, Jr.
Michael S. Costello
Conrod K. Cottoy
Martin John Coughlan
John Gerard Coughlin
Timothy J. Coughlin
James E. Cove
Andre Cox
Frederick John Cox
James Raymond Coyle
Michele Coyle-Eulau
Anne Marie Cramer
Christopher S. Cramer
Denise Elizabeth Crant
James Leslie Crawford, Jr.
Robert James Crawford
Joanne Mary Cregan
Lucy Crifasi
John A. Crisci
Daniel Hal Crisman
Dennis Cross
Kevin Raymond Crotty
Thomas G. Crotty
John Crowe
Welles Remy Crowther
Robert L. Cruikshank
John Robert Cruz
Grace Yu Cua
Kenneth John Cubas
Francisco Cruz Cubero
Richard J. Cudina

Neil James Cudmore
Thomas Patrick Cullen lll
Joyce Cummings
Brian Thomas Cummins
Michael Cunningham
Robert Curatolo
Laurence Damian Curia
Paul Dario Curioli
Beverly Curry
Michael S. Curtin
Gavin Cushny
John D'Allara
Vincent Gerard D'Amadeo
Jack D'Ambrosi
Mary D'Antonio
Edward A. D'Atri
Michael D. D'Auria
Michael Jude D'Esposito
Manuel John Da Mota
Caleb Arron Dack
Carlos S. DaCosta
Joao Alberto DaFonseca Aguiar, Jr.
Thomas A. Damaskinos
Jeannine Marie Damiani-Jones
Patrick W. Danahy
Nana Danso
Vincent Danz
Dwight Donald Darcy
Elizabeth Ann Darling
Annette Andrea Dataram
Lawrence Davidson
Michael Allen Davidson
Scott Matthew Davidson
Titus Davidson
Niurka Davila
Clinton Davis
Wayne Terrial Davis
Anthony Richard Dawson
Calvin Dawson
Edward James Day
Jayceryll de Chavez
Jennifer De Jesus
Monique E. De Jesus
Nereida De Jesus
Emerita De La Pena
Azucena Maria de la Torre
David Paul De Rubbio
Jemal Legesse De Santis
Christian Louis De Simone
Melanie Louise De Vere
William Thomas Dean
Robert J. DeAngelis, Jr.
Thomas Patrick DeAngelis
Tara E. Debek
Anna Marjia DeBin
James V. Deblase
Paul DeCola
Simon Marash Dedvukaj
Jason Defazio
David A. DeFeo
Manuel Del Valle, Jr.
Donald Arthur Delapenha
Vito Joseph DeLeo
Danielle Anne Delie

Joseph A. Della Pietra
Andrea DellaBella
Palmina DelliGatti
Colleen Ann Deloughery
Francis Albert DeMartini
Anthony Demas
Martin N. DeMeo
Francis Deming
Carol K. Demitz
Kevin Dennis
Thomas F. Dennis
Jean DePalma
Jose Depena
Robert John Deraney
Michael DeRienzo
Edward DeSimone III
Andrew Desperito
Cindy Ann Deuel
Jerry DeVito
Robert P. Devitt, Jr.
Dennis Lawrence Devlin
Gerard Dewan
Sulemanali Kassamali Dhanani
Patricia Florence Di Chiaro
Debra Ann Di Martino
Michael Louis Diagostino
Matthew Diaz
Nancy Diaz
Rafael Arturo Diaz
Michael A. Diaz-Piedra III
Judith Berquis Diaz-Sierra
Joseph Dermot Dickey, Jr.
Lawrence Patrick Dickinson
Michael D. Diehl
John Difato
Vincent Difazio
Carl Anthony DiFranco
Donald Difranco
Stephen Patrick Dimino
William John Dimmling
Marisa DiNardo Schorpp
Christopher M. Dincuff
Jeffrey Mark Dingle
Anthony Dionisio
George DiPasquale
Joseph Dipilato
Douglas Frank DiStefano
Ramzi A. Doany
John Joseph Doherty
Melissa C. Doi
Brendan Dolan
Neil Matthew Dollard
James Joseph Domanico
Benilda Pascua Domingo
Carlos Dominguez
Jerome Mark Patrick Dominguez
Kevin W. Donnelly
Jacqueline Donovan
Stephen Scott Dorf
Thomas Dowd
Kevin Dowdell
Mary Yolanda Dowling
Raymond Mathew Downey
Frank Joseph Doyle

Joseph Michael Doyle
Stephen Patrick Driscoll
Mirna A. Duarte
Michelle Beale Duberry
Luke A. Dudek
Christopher Michael Duffy
Gerard Duffy
Michael Joseph Duffy
Thomas W. Duffy
Antoinette Duger
Sareve Dukat
Christopher Joseph Dunne
Richard Anthony Dunstan
Patrick Thomas Dwyer
Joseph Anthony Eacobacci
John Bruce Eagleson
Robert Douglas Eaton
Dean Phillip Eberling
Margaret Ruth Echtermann
Paul Robert Eckna
Constantine Economos
Dennis Michael Edwards
Michael Hardy Edwards
Christine Egan
Lisa Egan
Martin J. Egan, Jr.
Michael Egan
Samantha Martin Egan
Carole Eggert
Lisa Caren Ehrlich
John Ernst Eichler
Eric Adam Eisenberg
Daphne Ferlinda Elder
Michael J. Elferis
Mark Joseph Ellis
Valerie Silver Ellis
Albert Alfy William Elmarry
Edgar Hendricks Emery, Jr.
Doris Suk-Yuen Eng
Christopher Epps
Ulf Ramm Ericson
Erwin L. Erker
William John Erwin
Jose Espinal
Fanny Espinoza
Bridget Ann Esposito
Francis Esposito
Michael Esposito
William Esposito
Ruben Esquilin, Jr.
Sadie Ette
Barbara G. Etzold
Eric Brian Evans
Robert Evans
Meredith Emily June Ewart
Catherine K. Fagan
Patricia Mary Fagan
Keith George Fairben
Sandra Fajardo-Smith
William F. Fallon
William Lawrence Fallon, Jr.
Anthony J. Fallone, Jr.
Dolores Brigitte Fanelli
John Joseph Fanning

Kathleen Anne Faragher
Thomas Farino
Nancy Carole Farley
Elizabeth Ann Farmer
Douglas Jon Farnum
John G. Farrell
John W. Farrell
Terrence Patrick Farrell
Joseph D. Farrelly
Thomas Patrick Farrelly
Syed Abdul Fatha
Christopher Edward Faughnan
Wendy R. Faulkner
Shannon Marie Fava
Bernard D. Favuzza
Robert Fazio, Jr.
Ronald Carl Fazio
William Feehan
Francis Jude Feely
Garth Erin Feeney
Sean B. Fegan
Lee S. Fehling
Peter Adam Feidelberg
Alan D. Feinberg
Rosa Maria Feliciano
Edward Thomas Fergus, Jr.
George Ferguson
Henry Fernandez
Judy Hazel Fernandez
Julio Fernandez
Elisa Giselle Ferraina
Anne Marie Sallerin Ferreira
Robert John Ferris
David Francis Ferrugio
Louis V. Fersini
Michael David Ferugio
Bradley James Fetchet
Jennifer Louise Fialko
Kristen Nicole Fiedel
Samuel Fields
Michael Bradley Finnegan
Timothy J. Finnerty
Michael Curtis Fiore
Stephen S R Fiorelli, Sr.
Paul M. Fiori
John B. Fiorito
John R. Fischer
Andrew Fisher
Bennett Lawson Fisher
John Roger Fisher
Thomas J. Fisher
Lucy A. Fishman
Ryan D. Fitzgerald
Thomas James Fitzpatrick
Richard P. Fitzsimons
Salvatore Fiumefreddo
Christina Donovan Flannery
Eileen Flecha
Andre G. Fletcher
Carl M. Flickinger
John Joseph Florio
Joseph Walken Flounders
David Fodor
Michael N. Fodor

Stephen Mark Fogel
Thomas Foley
David J. Fontana
Chih Min Foo
Godwin Forde
Donald A. Foreman
Christopher Hugh Forsythe
Claudia Alicia Foster
Noel John Foster
Ana Fosteris
Robert Joseph Foti
Jeffrey Fox
Virginia Fox
Pauline Francis
Virgin Francis
Gary Jay Frank
Morton H. Frank
Peter Christopher Frank
Richard K. Fraser
Kevin J. Frawley
Clyde Frazier, Jr.
Lillian Inez Frederick
Andrew Fredricks
Tamitha Freeman
Brett Owen Freiman
Peter L. Freund
Arlene Eva Fried
Alan Wayne Friedlander
Andrew Keith Friedman
Gregg J. Froehner
Peter Christian Fry
Clement A. Fumando
Steven Elliot Furman
Paul Furmato
Fredric Neal Gabler
Richard Samuel Federick Gabrielle
James Andrew Gadiel
Pamela Lee Gaff
Ervin Vincent Gailliard
Deanna Lynn Galante
Grace Catherine Galante
Anthony Edward Gallagher
Daniel James Gallagher
John Patrick Gallagher
Lourdes Galletti
Cono E. Gallo
Vincenzo Gallucci
Thomas E. Galvin
Giovanna Galletta Gambale
Thomas Gambino, Jr.
Giann Franco Gamboa
Peter Ganci
Ladkat K. Ganesh
Claude Michael Gann
Osseni Garba
Charles William Garbarini
Ceasar Garcia
David Garcia
Juan Garcia
Marlyn Del Carmen Garcia
Christopher S. Gardner
Douglas Benjamin Gardner
Harvey J. Gardner III
Jeffrey Brian Gardner

Thomas Gardner
William Arthur Gardner
Francesco Garfi
Rocco Nino Gargano
James M. Gartenberg
Matthew David Garvey
Bruce Gary
Boyd Alan Gatton
Donald Richard Gavagan, Jr.
Terence D. Gazzani
Gary Geidel
Paul Hamilton Geier
Julie M. Geis
Peter G. Gelinas
Steven Paul Geller
Howard G. Gelling
Peter Victor Genco, Jr.
Steven Gregory Genovese
Alayne Gentul
Edward F. Geraghty
Suzanne Geraty
Ralph Gerhardt
Robert Gerlich
Denis P. Germain
Marina Romanovna Gertsberg
Susan M. Getzendanner
James G. Geyer
Joseph M. Giaccone
Vincent Francis Giammona
Debra Lynn Gibbon
James Andrew Giberson
Craig Neil Gibson
Ronnie E. Gies
Laura A. Giglio
Andrew Clive Gilbert
Timothy Paul Gilbert
Paul Stuart Gilbey
Paul John Gill
Mark Y. Gilles
Evan Gillette
Ronald Lawrence Gilligan
Rodney C. Gillis
Laura Gilly
John F. Ginley
Donna Marie Giordano
Jeffrey John Giordano
John Giordano
Steven A. Giorgetti
Martin Giovinazzo
Kum-Kum Girolamo
Salvatore Gitto
Cynthia Giugliano
Mon Gjonbalaj
Dianne Gladstone
Keith Glascoe
Thomas Irwin Glasser
Harry Glenn
Barry H. Glick
Steven Glick
John T. Gnazzo
William Robert Godshalk
Michael Gogliormella
Brian Fredric Goldberg
Jeffrey Grant Goldflam

Michelle Goldstein
Monica Goldstein
Steven Goldstein
Andrew H. Golkin
Dennis James Gomes
Enrique Antonio Gomez
Jose Bienvenido Gomez
Manuel Gomez, Jr.
Wilder Alfredo Gomez
Jenine Nicole Gonzalez
Mauricio Gonzalez
Rosa Gonzalez
Calvin J. Gooding
Harry Goody
Kiran Reddy Gopu
Catherine C. Gorayeb
Kerene Gordon
Sebastian Gorki
Kieran Joseph Gorman
Thomas Edward Gorman
Michael Edward Gould
Yuji Goya
Jon Richard Grabowski
Christopher Michael Grady
Edwin J. Graf III
David Martin Graifman
Gilbert Franco Granados
Elvira Granitto
Winston Arthur Grant
Christopher S. Gray
James Michael Gray
Tara McCloud Gray
Linda Catherine Grayling
John M. Grazioso
Timothy George Grazioso
Derrick Auther Green
Wade B. Green
Elaine Myra Greenberg
Gayle R. Greene
James Arthur Greenleaf, Jr.
Eileen Marsha Greenstein
Elizabeth Martin Gregg
Denise Gregory
Donald H. Gregory
Florence Moran Gregory
Pedro Grehan
John Michael Griffin
Tawanna Sherry Griffin
Joan Donna Griffith
Warren Grifka
Ramon Grijalvo
Joseph F. Grillo
David Joseph Grimner
Kenneth George Grouzalis
Joseph Grzelak
Matthew James Grzymalski
Robert Joseph Gschaar
Liming Gu
Jose Guadalupe
Cindy Yan Zhu Guan
Joel Guevara Gonzalez
Geoffrey E. Guja
Joseph Gullickson
Babita Girjamatie Guman

Douglas Brian Gurian
Janet Ruth Gustafson
Philip T. Guza
Barbara Guzzardo
Peter M. Gyulavary
Gary Robert Haag
Andrea Lyn Haberman
Barbara Mary Habib
Philip Haentzler
Nezam A. Hafiz
Karen Elizabeth Hagerty
Steven Michael Hagis
Mary Lou Hague
David Halderman
Maile Rachel Hale
Richard B. Hall
Vaswald George Hall
Robert J. Halligan
Vincent Gerard Halloran
James Douglas Halvorson
Mohammad Salman Hamdani
Felicia Hamilton
Robert Hamilton
Frederic K. Han
Christopher J. Hanley
Sean S. Hanley
Valerie Joan Hanna
Thomas Hannafin
Kevin James Hannaford
Michael Lawrence Hannan
Dana R Hannon
Vassilios G. Haramis
James A. Haran
Jeffrey Pike Hardy
Timothy John Hargrave
Daniel Edward Harlin
Frances Haros
Harvey Harrell
Stephen G. Harrell
Melissa Marie Harrington
Aisha Anne Harris
Stewart Dennis Harris
John Patrick Hart
John Clinton Hartz
Emeric Harvey
Thomas Theodore Haskell, Jr.
Timothy Haskell
Joseph John Hasson III
Leonard W. Hatton
Terence S. Hatton
Michael Haub
Timothy Aaron Haviland
Donald G. Havlish, Jr.
Anthony Hawkins
Nobuhiro Hayatsu
Philip Hayes
William Ward Haynes
Scott Jordan Hazelcorn
Michael K. Healey
Roberta B. Heber
Charles Francis Xavier Heeran
John F. Heffernan
H. Joseph Heller, Jr.
Joann L. Heltibridle

Mark F. Hemschoot
Ronnie Lee Henderson
Brian Hennessey
Michelle Marie Henrique
Joseph Henry
William Henry
John Christopher Henwood
Robert Allan Hepburn
Mary Herencia
Lindsay C. Herkness III
Harvey Robert Hermer
Claribel Hernandez
Eduardo Hernandez
Nuberto Hernandez
Raul Hernandez
Gary Herold
Jeffrey A. Hersch
Thomas Hetzel
Brian Hickey
Ysidro Hidalgo
Timothy Higgins
Robert D. W. Higley II
Todd Russell Hill
Clara Victorine Hinds
Neal O. Hinds
Mark D. Hindy
Katsuyuki Hirai
Heather Malia Ho
Tara Yvette Hobbs
Thomas Anderson Hobbs
James J. Hobin
Robert Wayne Hobson
DaJuan Hodges
Ronald George Hoerner
Patrick A. Hoey
Marcia Hoffman
Stephen G. Hoffman
Frederick Joseph Hoffmann
Michele L. Hoffmann
Judith Florence Hofmiller
Thomas Warren Hohlweck, Jr.
Jonathan R. Hohmann
John Holland
Joseph F. Holland
Elizabeth Holmes
Thomas Holohan
Bradley Hoorn
James P. Hopper
Montgomery McCullough Hord
Michael Horn
Matthew Douglas Horning
Robert L. Horohoe, Jr.
Aaron Horwitz
Charles Houston
Uhuru G. Houston
George Howard
Michael C. Howell
Steven Leon Howell
Jennifer L. Howley
Milagros Hromada
Marian R. Hrycak
Stephen Huczko, Jr.
Kris Robert Hughes
Paul Rexford Hughes

Robert Thomas Hughes
Thomas Hughes
Timothy Robert Hughes
Susan Huie
Lamar Hulse
William Christopher Hunt
Kathleen Anne Hunt-Casey
Joseph Hunter
Robert R. Hussa
Abid Hussain
Thomas Edward Hynes
Walter G. Hynes
Joseph Anthony Ianelli
Zuhtu Ibis
Jonathan Lee Ielpi
Michael Iken
Daniel Ilkanayev
Frederick Ill, Jr.
Abraham Nethanel Ilowitz
Anthony P. Infante, Jr.
Louis S. Inghilterra, Jr.
Christopher Noble Ingrassia
Paul Innella
Stephanie Veronica Irby
Douglas Irgang
Kristin A. Irvine Ryan
Todd Antione Isaac
Erik Isbrandtsen
Taizo Ishikawa
Aram Iskenderian, Jr.
John F. Iskyan
Kazushige Ito
Aleksandr Valeryevich Ivantsov
Virginia May Jablonski
Brooke Alexandra Jackman
Aaron Jeremy Jacobs
Ariel Louis Jacobs
Jason Kyle Jacobs
Michael Grady Jacobs
Steven A. Jacobson
Ricknauth Jaggernauth
Jake Denis Jagoda
Yudh Vir Singh Jain
Maria Jakubiak
Ernest James
Gricelda E. James
Priscilla James
Mark Steven Jardim
Muhammadou Jawara
Francois Jean-Pierre
Maxima Jean-Pierre
Paul Edward Jeffers
Alva Cynthia Jeffries Sanchez
Joseph Jenkins, Jr.
Alan Keith Jensen
Prem N. Jerath
Farah Jeudy
Hweidar Jian
Eliezer Jimenez, Jr.
Luis Jimenez, Jr.
Fernando Jimenez-Molina
Charles Gregory John
Nicholas John
LaShawna Johnson

Scott Michael Johnson
William R. Johnston
Allison Horstmann Jones
Arthur Joseph Jones
Brian Leander Jones
Christopher D. Jones
Donald T. Jones
Donald W. Jones
Linda Jones
Mary S. Jones
Andrew Jordan
Robert Thomas Jordan
Albert Gunnia Joseph
Guylene Joseph
Ingeborg Joseph
Karl Henry Joseph
Stephen Joseph
Jane Eileen Josiah
Anthony Jovic
Angel L. Juarbe, Jr.
Karen Sue Juday
Mychal F. Judge
Paul William Jurgens
Thomas Edward Jurgens
Kacinga Kabeya
Shashikiran Lakshmikantha Kadaba
Gavkharoy Kamardinova
Shari Kandell
Howard Lee Kane
Jennifer Lynn Kane
Vincent D. Kane
Joon Koo Kang
Sheldon Robert Kanter
Deborah H. Kaplan
Alvin Peter Kappelmann, Jr.
Charles Karczewski
William A. Karnes
Douglas Gene Karpiloff
Charles L. Kasper
Andrew K. Kates
John Katsimatides
Robert Michael Kaulfers
Don Jerome Kauth, Jr.
Hideya Kawauchi
Edward T. Keane
Richard M. Keane
Lisa Yvonne Kearney-Griffin
Karol Ann Keasler
Paul Hanlon Keating
Leo Russell Keene III
Joseph John Keller
Peter R. Kellerman
Joseph P. Kellett
Frederick H. Kelley, Jr.
James Joseph Kelly
Joseph A. Kelly
Maurice P. Kelly
Richard John Kelly, Jr.
Thomas Michael Kelly
Thomas Richard Kelly
Thomas W. Kelly
Timothy Colin Kelly
William Hill Kelly, Jr.
Robert Clinton Kennedy

Thomas J. Kennedy
John R. Keohane
Ronald T. Kerwin
Howard L. Kestenbaum
Douglas D. Ketcham
Ruth Ellen Ketler
Boris Khalif
Sarah Khan
Taimour Firaz Khan
Rajesh Khandelwal
Oliva Khemrat
SeiLai Khoo
Michael Kiefer
Satoshi Kikuchihara
Andrew Jay-Hoon Kim
Lawrence D. Kim
Mary Jo Kimelman
Andrew M. King
Lucille Teresa King
Robert King, Jr.
Lisa King-Johnson
Takashi Kinoshita
Chris Michael Kirby
Howard Barry Kirschbaum
Glenn Davis Kirwin
Helen Crossin Kittle
Richard Joseph Klares
Peter Anton Klein
Alan David Kleinberg
Karen Joyce Klitzman
Ronald Philip Kloepfer
Evgueni Kniazev
Andrew Knox
Thomas Patrick Knox
Rebecca Lee Koborie
Deborah A. Kobus
Gary Edward Koecheler
Frank J. Koestner
Ryan Kohart
Vanessa Kolpak
Irina Kolpakova
Suzanne Kondratenko
Abdoulaye Kone
Bon-Seok Koo
Dorota Kopiczko
Scott Kopytko
Bojan Kostic
Danielle Kousoulis
John J. Kren
William E. Krukowski
Lyudmila Ksido
Shekhar Kumar
Kenneth Kumpel
Frederick Kuo, Jr.
Patricia Kuras
Nauka Kushitani
Thomas Kuveikis
Victor Kwarkye
Kui Fai Kwok
Angela Reed Kyte
Andrew La Corte
Amarnauth Lachhman
James Patrick Ladley
Joseph A. LaFalce

Jeanette Louise Lafond-Menichino
David Laforge
Michael Laforte
Alan Charles LaFrance
Juan Lafuente
Neil Kwong-Wah Lai
Vincent Anthony Laieta
William David Lake
Franco Lalama
Chow Kwan Lam
Stephen LaMantia
Amy Hope Lamonsoff
Nickola Lampley
Robert Lane
Brendan Mark Lang
Rosanne P. Lang
Vanessa Langer
Mary Louise Langley
Peter J. Langone
Thomas Michael Langone
Michele Bernadette Lanza
Ruth Sheila Lapin
Carol Ann LaPlante
Ingeborg Lariby
Robin Blair Larkey
Christopher Randall Larrabee
Hamidou S. Larry
Scott Larsen
John Adam Larson
Gary Edward Lasko
Nicholas Craig Lassman
Paul Laszczynski
Jeffrey G. LaTouche
Charles Laurencin
Stephen James Lauria
Maria LaVache
Denis Francis Lavelle
Jeannine Mary LaVerde
Anna A. Laverty
Steven Lawn
Robert Lawrence
Nathaniel Lawson
Eugen Gabriel Lazar
James Patrick Leahy
Joseph Gerard Leavey
Neil Joseph Leavy
Leon Lebor
Kenneth Charles Ledee
Alan J. Lederman
Elena F. Ledesma
Alexis Leduc
David S. Lee
Gary H. Lee
Hyun Joon Lee
Juanita Lee
Kathryn Blair Lee
Linda C. Lee
Lorraine Mary Lee
Myoung Woo Lee
Richard Y. Lee
Stuart Soo-Jin Lee
Yang Der Lee
Stephen Paul Lefkowitz
Adriana Legro

Edward Joseph Lehman
Eric Andrew Lehrfeld
David Leistman
David Prudencio Lemagne
Joseph Anthony Lenihan
John Joseph Lennon, Jr.
John Robinson Lenoir
Jorge Luis Leon
Matthew Gerard Leonard
Michael Lepore
Charles A. Lesperance
Jeff Leveen
John Dennis Levi
Alisha Caren Levin
Neil David Levin
Robert Levine
Robert Michael Levine
Shai Levinhar
Adam Jay Lewis
Margaret Susan Lewis
Ye Wei Liang
Orasri Liangthanasarn
Daniel F. Libretti
Ralph Licciardi
Edward Lichtschein
Steven Barry Lillianthal
Carlos R. Lillo
Craig Damian Lilore
Arnold A. Lim
Darya Lin
Wei Rong Lin
Nickie L. Lindo
Thomas V. Linehan, Jr.
Robert Thomas Linnane
Alan P. Linton, Jr.
Diane Theresa Lipari
Kenneth Lira
Francisco Alberto Liriano
Lorraine Lisi
Paul Lisson
Vincent M. Litto
Ming-Hao Liu
Nancy Liz
Harold Lizcano
Martin Lizzul
George A. Llanes
Elizabeth C. Logler
Catherine Lisa Loguidice
Jerome Robert Lohez
Michael William Lomax
Laura Maria Longing
Salvatore Lopes
Daniel Lopez
George Lopez
Luis Manuel Lopez
Manuel L. Lopez
Joseph Lostrangio
Chet Dek Louie
Stuart Seid Louis
Joseph Lovero
Jenny Seu Kueng Low Wong
Michael W. Lowe
Garry W. Lozier
John Peter Lozowsky

Charles Peter Lucania
Edward Hobbs Luckett
Mark Gavin Ludvigsen
Lee Charles Ludwig
Sean Thomas Lugano
Daniel Lugo
Marie Lukas
William Lum, Jr.
Michael P. Lunden
Christopher Lunder
Anthony Luparello
Gary Frederick Lutnick
William Lutz
Linda Anne Luzzicone
Alexander Lygin
Farrell Peter Lynch
James Francis Lynch
Louise A. Lynch
Michael Cameron Lynch
Michael F. Lynch
Michael Francis Lynch
Richard D. Lynch, Jr.
Robert Henry Lynch, Jr.
Sean P. Lynch
Sean Patrick Lynch
Michael J. Lyons
Monica Anne Lyons
Patrick Lyons
Robert Francis Mace
Jan Maciejewski
Catherine Fairfax Macrae
Richard Blaine Madden
Simon Maddison Noell Maerz
Jennieann Maffeo
Joseph Maffeo
Jay Robert Magazine
Brian Magee
Charles Wilson Magee
Joseph V. Maggitti
Ronald Magnuson
Daniel L. Maher
Thomas Anthony Mahon
William J. Mahoney
Joseph Daniel Maio
Takashi Makimoto
Abdu Ali Malahi
Debora I. Maldonado
Myrna T. Maldonado-Agosto
Alfred Russell Maler
Gregory James Malone
Edward Francis Maloney III
Joseph Maloney
Gene Edward Maloy
Christian Maltby
Francisco Miguel Mancini
Joseph Mangano
Sara Elizabeth Manley
Debra Mannetta
Marion Victoria Manning
Terence John Manning
James Maounis
Joseph Ross Marchbanks, Jr.
Peter Edward Mardikian
Edward Joseph Mardovich

Charles Joseph Margiotta
Kenneth Joseph Marino
Lester V. Marino
Vita Marino
Kevin Marlo
Jose Marrero
John Marshall
James Martello
Michael A. Marti
Peter C. Martin
William J. Martin, Jr.
Brian E. Martineau
Betsy Martinez
Edward Martinez
Jose Angel Martinez, Jr.
Robert Gabriel Martinez
Victor Martinez Pastrana
Lizie D. Martinez-Calderon
Paul Richard Martini
Joseph A. Mascali
Bernard Mascarenhas
Stephen Frank Masi
Nicholas George Massa
Patricia Ann Massari
Michael Massaroli
Philip William Mastrandrea, Jr.
Rudolph Mastrocinque
Joseph Mathai
Charles Mathers
William A. Mathesen
Marcello Matricciano
Margaret Elaine Mattic
Robert D. Mattson
Walter Matuza
Charles A. Mauro, Jr.
Charles J. Mauro
Dorothy Mauro
Nancy T. Mauro
Tyrone May
Keithroy Marcellus Maynard
Robert J. Mayo
Kathy Nancy Mazza
Edward Mazzella, Jr.
Jennifer Lynn Mazzotta
Kaaria Mbaya
James Joseph McAlary
Brian McAleese
Patricia Ann McAneney
Colin Robert McArthur
John Kevin McAvoy
Kenneth M. McBrayer
Brendan McCabe
Micheal McCabe
Thomas McCann
Justin McCarthy
Kevin M. McCarthy
Michael McCarthy
Robert McCarthy
Stanley McCaskill
Katie Marie McCloskey
Joan McConnell-Cullinan
Charles Austin McCrann
Tonyell F. McDay
Matthew T. McDermott

Joseph P. McDonald
Brian Grady McDonnell
Michael P. McDonnell
John McDowell, Jr.
Eamon J. McEneaney
John Thomas McErlean, Jr.
Daniel Francis McGinley
Mark Ryan McGinly
William E. McGinn
Thomas Henry MCGinnis
Michael Gregory McGinty
Ann McGovern
Scott Martin McGovern
William McGovern
Stacey Sennas McGowan
Francis Noel McGuinn
Patrick McGuire
Thomas M. McHale
Keith McHeffey
Ann M. McHugh
Denis J. McHugh III
Dennis McHugh
Michael E. McHugh
Robert G. McIlvaine
Donald James McIntyre
Stephanie Marie McKenna
Barry J. McKeon
Evelyn C. McKinnedy
Darryl Leron McKinney
George Patrick McLaughlin, Jr.
Robert C. McLaughlin, Jr.
Gavin McMahon
Robert D. McMahon
Edmund McNally
Daniel W. McNeal
Walter Arthur McNeil
Jisley McNish
Christine Sheila McNulty
Sean Peter McNulty
Robert McPadden
Terence A. McShane
Timothy Patrick McSweeney
Martin E. McWilliams
Rocco A. Medaglia
Abigail Cales Medina
Ana Iris Medina
Deborah Louise Medwig
Damian Meehan
William J. Meehan
Alok Mehta
Raymond Meisenheimer
Manuel Emilio Mejia
Eskedar Melaku
Antonio Melendez
Mary Melendez
Yelena Melnichenko
Stuart Todd Meltzer
Diarelia Jovanah Mena
Charles Mendez
Lizette Mendoza
Shevonne Olicia Mentis
Steven Mercado
Westly Mercer
Ralph Joseph Mercurio

Alan Harvey Merdinger
George L. Merino
Yamel Merino
George Merkouris
Deborah Merrick
Raymond Joseph Metz III
Jill Ann Metzler
David Robert Meyer
Nurul H. Miah
William Edward Micciulli
Martin Paul Michelstein
Peter Teague Milano
Gregory Milanowycz
Lukasz Tomasz Milewski
Sharon Christina Millan
Corey Peter Miller
Craig James Miller
Douglas Charles Miller
Henry Alfred Miller, Jr.
Joel Miller
Michael Matthew Miller
Philip D. Miller
Robert Alan Miller
Robert Cromwell Miller, Jr.
Benjamin Millman
Charles Morris Mills
Ronald Keith Milstein
Robert Minara
William George Minardi
Diakite Minata
Louis Joseph Minervino
Thomas Mingione
Wilbert Miraille
Dominick N. Mircovich
Rajesh Arjan Mirpuri
Joseph Mistrulli
Susan J. Miszkowicz
Paul Thomas Mitchell
Richard P. Miuccio
Frank V. Moccia, Sr.
Louis Joseph Modafferi
Boyie Mohammed
Dennis Mojica
Manuel Mojica
Kleber Molina
Manuel De Jesus Molina
Carl Molinaro
Justin Molisani
Brian Monaghan
Franklin Monahan
John Monahan
Kristen Montanaro
Craig Montano
Michael Montesi
Jeffrey Montgomery
Peter Montoulieu
Cheryl Ann Monyak
Thomas Moody
Sharon Moore
Krishna Moorthy
Abner Morales
Carlos Manuel Morales
Luis Morales
Paula E. Morales John Moran

John Chrisopher Moran
Kathleen Moran
Lindsay Stapleton Morehouse
George Morell
Steven P. Morello
Vincent S. Morello
Yvette Nicole Moreno
Dorothy Morgan
Richard Morgan
Nancy Morgenstern
Sanae Mori
Blanca Robertina Morocho
Leonel Geronimo Morocho
Dennis Gerard Moroney
Lynne Irene Morris
Seth Allan Morris
Stephen Philip Morris
Christopher Martel Morrison
Jorge Luis Morron Garcia
Ferdinand V. Morrone
William David Moskal
Marco Motroni
Cynthia Motus-Wilson
Iouri A. Mouchinski
Jude Joseph Moussa
Peter Moutos
Damion O'Neil Mowatt
Christopher Mozzillo
Stephen Vincent Mulderry
Richard Muldowney Jr
Michael D. Mullan
Dennis Michael Mulligan
Peter James Mulligan
Michael Joseph Mullin
James Donald Munhall
Nancy Muniz
Carlos Munoz
Frank Munoz
Theresa Munson
Robert M. Murach
Cesar Augusto Murillo
Marc A. Murolo
Brian Joseph Murphy
Charles Anthony Murphy
Christopher W. Murphy
Edward Charles Murphy
James F. Murphy Iv
James Thomas Murphy
Kevin James Murphy
Patrick Sean Murphy
Raymond E. Murphy
Robert Eddie Murphy, Jr.
John Joseph Murray
John Joseph Murray, Jr.
Susan D. Murray
Valerie Victoria Murray
Richard Todd Myhre
Robert B. Nagel
Takuya Nakamura
Alexander Napier
Frank Joseph Naples III
John Napolitano
Catherine Ann Nardella
Mario Nardone, Jr.

Manika K. Narula
Mehmood Naseem
Narender Nath
Karen Susan Navarro
Joseph Micheal Navas
Francis Joseph Nazario
Glenroy I. Neblett
Rayman Marcus Neblett
Jerome O. Nedd
Laurence Nedell
Luke G. Nee
Pete Negron
Ann N. Nelson
David William Nelson
James Nelson
Michele Ann Nelson
Peter Allen Nelson
Oscar Francis Nesbitt
Gerard Terence Nevins
Christopher Newton-Carter
Kapinga Ngalula
Nancy Yuen Ngo
Jody Nichilo
Martin S. Niederer
Alfonse Joseph Niedermeyer
Frank John Niestadt, Jr.
Gloria Nieves
Juan Nieves, Jr.
Troy Edward Nilsen
Paul Nimbley
John B. Niven
Katherine Marie Noack
Curtis Terrance Noel
Daniel R. Nolan
Robert Noonan
Daniela R. Notaro
Brian Christopher Novotny
Soichi Numata
Brian Felix Nunez
Jose Nunez
Jeffrey Roger Nussbaum
Dennis O'Berg
James P. O'Brien, Jr.
Michael P. O'Brien
Scott J. O'Brien
Timothy Michael O'Brien
Daniel O'Callaghan
Dennis James O'Connor, Jr.
Diana J. O'Connor
Keith Kevin O'Connor
Richard J. O'Connor
Amy O'Doherty
Marni Pont O'Doherty
James Andrew O'Grady
Thomas O'Hagan
Patrick J. O'Keefe
William O'Keefe
Gerald O'leary
Matthew Timothy O'Mahony
Peter J. O'Neill, Jr.
Sean Gordon O'Neill
Kevin O'Rourke
Patrick J. O'Shea
Robert William O'Shea

Timothy F. O'Sullivan
James A. Oakley
Douglas E. Oelschlager
Takashi Ogawa
Albert Ogletree
Philip Paul Ognibene
Joseph J. Ogren
Samuel Oitice
Gerald Michael Olcott
Christine Anne Olender
Linda Mary Oliva
Edward Kraft Oliver
Leah E. Oliver
Eric T. Olsen
Jeffrey James Olsen
Maureen Lyons Olson
Steven John Olson
Toshihiro Onda
Seamus L. O'Neal
John P. Oneill
Frank Oni
Michael C. Opperman
Christopher Orgielewicz
Margaret Orloske
Virginia Anne Ormiston
Ronald Orsini
Peter Ortale
Juan Ortega-Campos
Alexander Ortiz
David Ortiz
Emilio Ortiz, Jr.
Pablo Ortiz
Paul Ortiz, Jr.
Sonia Ortiz
Masaru Ose
Elsy C. Osorio
James R. Ostrowski
Jason Douglas Oswald
Michael Otten
Isidro D. Ottenwalder
Michael Chung Ou
Todd Joseph Ouida
Jesus Ovalles
Peter J. Owens, Jr.
Adianes Oyola
Angel M. Pabon
Israel Pabon, Jr.
Roland Pacheco
Michael Benjamin Packer
Rene Padilla-Chavarria
Deepa Pakkala
Jeffrey Matthew Palazzo
Thomas Palazzo
Richard Palazzolo
Orio J. Palmer
Frank Anthony Palombo
Alan N. Palumbo
Christopher Matthew Panatier
Dominique Lisa Pandolfo
Paul J. Pansini
John M. Paolillo
Edward Joseph Papa
Salvatore T. Papasso
James Nicholas Pappageorge

Vinod Kumar Parakat
Vijayashanker Paramsothy
Nitin Parandkar
Hardai Parbhu
James Wendell Parham
Debra Marie Paris
George Paris
Gye Hyong Park
Philip Lacey Parker
Michael Alaine Parkes
Robert E. Parks, Jr.
Hashmukhrai C. Parmar
Robert Parro
Diane Marie Parsons
Leobardo Lopez Pascual
Michael Pascuma
Jerrold Paskins
Horace Robert Passananti
Suzanne H. Passaro
Avnish Ramanbhai Patel
Dipti Patel
Manish Patel
Steven Bennett Paterson
James Matthew Patrick
Manuel D. Patrocino
Bernard E. Patterson
Cira Marie Patti
Robert E. Pattison
James Robert Paul
Patrice Paz
Victor Paz-Gutierrez
Stacey Lynn Peak
Richard Allen Pearlman
Durrell V. Pearsall
Thomas Pedicini
Todd Douglas Pelino
Michel Adrian Pelletier
Anthony G. Peluso
Angel Ramon Pena
Richard Al Penny
Salvatore F. Pepe
Carl Peralta
Robert David Peraza
Jon A. Perconti
Alejo Perez
Angel Perez, Jr.
Angela Susan Perez
Anthony Perez
Ivan Perez
Nancy E. Perez
Joseph John Perroncino
Edward J. Perrotta
Emelda H. Perry
Glenn C. Perry
John William Perry
Franklin Allan Pershep
Danny Pesce
Michael John Pescherine
Davin Peterson
William Russell Peterson
Mark Petrocelli
Philip Scott Petti
Glen Kerrin Pettit
Dominick Pezzulo

Kaleen Elizabeth Pezzuti
Kevin Pfeifer
Tu-Anh Pham
Kenneth Phelan
Sneha Ann Philips
Gerard Phillips
Suzette Eugenia Piantieri
Ludwig John Picarro
Matthew M. Picerno
Joseph Oswald Pick
Christopher Pickford
Dennis J. Pierce
Bernard Pietronico
Nicholas P. Pietrunti
Theodoros Pigis
Susan Elizabeth Pinto
Joseph Piskadlo
Christopher Todd Pitman
Joshua Piver
Joseph Plumitallo
John Pocher
William Howard Pohlmann
Laurence Polatsch
Thomas H. Polhemus
Steve Pollicino
Susan M. Pollio
Joshua Iousa Poptean
Giovanna Porras
Anthony Portillo
James Edward Potorti
Daphne Pouletsos
Richard N. Poulos
Stephen Emanual Poulos
Brandon Jerome Powell
Shawn Edward Powell
Antonio Pratt
Gregory M. Preziose
Wanda Ivelisse Prince
Vincent Princiotta
Kevin Prior
Everett Martin Proctor III
Carrie Beth Progen
Sarah Prothero-Redheffer
David Lee Pruim
Richard Prunty
John Foster Puckett
Robert David Pugliese
Edward F. Pullis
Patricia Ann Puma
Hemanth Kumar Puttur
Edward R. Pykon
Christopher Quackenbush
Lars Peter Qualben
Lincoln Quappe
Beth Ann Quigley
Michael Quilty
James Francis Quinn
Ricardo J. Quinn
Carlos Quishpe-Cuaman
Carol Millicent Rabalais
Christopher Peter A. Racaniello
Leonard J. Ragaglia
Eugene Raggio
Laura Marie Ragonese-Snik

Michael Ragusa
Peter Frank Raimondi
Harry A. Raines
Ehtesham Raja
Valsa Raju
Edward Rall
Lukas Rambousek
Maria Ramirez
Harry Ramos
Vishnoo Ramsaroop
Lorenzo E. Ramzey
Alfred Todd Rancke
Adam David Rand
Jonathan C. Randall
Srinivasa Shreyas Ranganath
Anne T. Ransom
Faina Aronovna Rapoport
Robert A. Rasmussen
Amenia Rasool
Roger Mark Rasweiler
David Alan Rathkey
William Ralph Raub
Gerard P. Rauzi
Alexey Razuvaev
Gregory Reda
Michele Reed
Judith Ann Reese
Donald J. Regan
Robert M. Regan
Thomas Michael Regan
Christian Michael Otto Regenhard
Howard Reich
Gregg Reidy
James Brian Reilly
Kevin O. Reilly
Timothy E. Reilly
Joseph Reina, Jr.
Thomas Barnes Reinig
Frank Bennett Reisman
Joshua Scott Reiss
Karen Renda
John Armand Reo
Richard Cyril Rescorla
John Thomas Resta
Luis Clodoaldo Revilla
Eduvigis Reyes, Jr.
Bruce Albert Reynolds
John Frederick Rhodes
Francis Saverio Riccardelli
Rudolph N. Riccio
Ann Marie Riccoboni
David H. Rice
Eileen Mary Rice
Kenneth Frederick Rice III
Vernon Allan Richard
Claude Daniel Richards
Gregory David Richards
Michael Richards
Venesha Orintia Richards
James C. Riches
Alan Jay Richman
John M. Rigo
Theresa Risco
Rose Mary Riso

Moises N. Rivas
Joseph Rivelli
Carmen Alicia Rivera
Isaias Rivera
Juan William Rivera
Linda Ivelisse Rivera
David E. Rivers
Joseph R. Riverso
Paul V. Rizza
John Frank Rizzo
Stephen Louis Roach
Joseph Roberto
Leo Arthur Roberts
Michael Roberts
Michael Edward Roberts
Donald Walter Robertson, Jr.
Catherina Robinson
Jeffery Robinson
Michell Lee Jean Robotham
Donald A. Robson
Antonio A. Rocha
Raymond James Rocha
Laura Rockefeller
John Rodak
Antonio J. Rodrigues
Anthony Rodriguez
Carmen Milagros Rodriguez
Gregory Ernesto Rodriguez
Marsha A. Rodriguez
Mayra Valdes Rodriguez
Richard Rodriguez
David Bartolo Rodriguez-Vargas
Matthew Rogan
Karlie Barbara Rogers
Scott Williams Rohner
Keith Roma
Joseph M. Romagnolo
Efrain Romero, Sr.
Elvin Romero
Juan Romero
Orozco James A. Romito
Sean Paul Rooney
Eric Thomas Ropiteau
Aida Rosario
Angela Rosario
Wendy Alice Rosario Wakeford
Mark Rosen
Brooke David Rosenbaum
Linda Rosenbaum
Sheryl Lynn Rosenbaum
Lloyd Daniel Rosenberg
Mark Louis Rosenberg
Andrew Ira Rosenblum
Joshua M. Rosenblum
Joshua Alan Rosenthal
Richard David Rosenthal
Daniel Rosetti
Norman S. Rossinow
Nicholas P. Rossomando
Michael Craig Rothberg
Donna Marie Rothenberg
Nicholas Rowe
Timothy Alan Roy, Sr.
Paul G. Ruback

Ronald J. Ruben
Joanne Rubino
David M. Ruddle
Bart Joseph Ruggiere
Susan A. Ruggiero
Adam Keith Ruhalter
Gilbert Ruiz
Obdulio Ruiz Diaz
Stephen P. Russell
Steven Harris Russin
Michael Thomas Russo, Sr.
Wayne Alan Russo
Edward Ryan
John Joseph Ryan, Jr.
Jonathan Stephan Ryan
Matthew Lancelot Ryan
Tatiana Ryjova
Christina Sunga Ryook
Thierry Saada
Jason Elazar Sabbag
Thomas E. Sabella
Scott Saber
Joseph Francis Sacerdote
Neeraha Sadaranghgani
Mohammad Ali Sadeque
Francis John Sadocha
Jude Safi
Brock Joel Safronoff
Edward Saiya
John Patrick Salamone
Hernando Salas
Juan G. Salas
Esmerlin Antonio Salcedo
John Salvatore Salerno, Jr.
Richard L. Salinardi, Jr.
Wayne John Saloman
Nolbert Salomon
Catherine Patricia Salter
Frank Salvaterra
Paul Richard Salvio
Samuel Robert Salvo, Jr.
Rena Sam-Dinnoo
Carlos Alberto Samaniego
James Kenneth Samuel, Jr.
Michael San Phillip
Sylvia San Pio
Hugo M. Sanay
Erick Sanchez
Jacquelyn Patrice Sanchez
Eric M. Sand
Stacey Leigh Sanders
Herman S. Sandler
James Sands, Jr.
Ayleen J. Santiago
Kirsten Santiago
Maria Theresa Santillan
Susan Gayle Santo
Christopher Santora
John A. Santore
Mario L. Santoro
Rafael Humberto Santos
Rufino Conrado Flores Santos Iii
Jorge Octavio Santos Anaya
Kalyan Sarkar

Chapelle R. Sarker
Paul F. Sarle
Deepika Kumar Sattaluri
Gregory Thomas Saucedo
Susan M. Sauer
Anthony Savas
Vladimir Savinkin
Jackie Sayegh
John Michael Sbarbaro
Robert L. Scandole, Jr.
Michelle Scarpitta
Dennis Scauso
John Albert Schardt
John G. Scharf
Frederick Claude Scheffold, Jr.
Angela Susan Scheinberg
Scott Mitchell Schertzer
Sean Schielke
Steven Francis Schlag
Jon Schlissel
Karen Helene Schmidt
Ian Schneider
Thomas G. Schoales
Frank G. Schott, Jr.
Gerard Patrick Schrang
Jeffrey H. Schreier
John T. Schroeder
Susan Lee Schuler
Edward William Schunk
Mark E. Schurmeier
Clarin Shellie Schwartz
John Burkhart Schwartz
Mark Schwartz
Adriane Victoria Scibetta
Raphael Scorca
Randolph Scott
Sheila Scott
Christopher Jay Scudder
Arthur Warren Scullin
Michael Herman Seaman
Margaret M. Seeliger
Anthony Segarra
Carlos Segarra
Jason Sekzer
Matthew Carmen Sellitto
Howard Selwyn
Larry John Senko
Arturo Angelo Sereno
Frankie Serrano
Alena Sesinova
Adele Christine Sessa
Sita Nermalla Sewnarine
Karen Lynn Seymour
Davis Sezna
Thomas Joseph Sgroi
Jayesh S. Shah
Khalid M. Shahid
Mohammed Shajahan
Gary Shamay
Earl Richard Shanahan
Neil Shastri
Kathryn Anne Shatzoff
Barbara A. Shaw
Jeffrey James Shaw

Robert John Shay, Jr.
Daniel James Shea
Joseph Patrick Shea
Linda Sheehan
Hagay Shefi
John Anthony Sherry
Atsushi Shiratori
Thomas Joseph Shubert
Mark Shulman
See Wong Shum
Allan Abraham Shwartzstein
Johanna Sigmund
Dianne T. Signer
Gregory Sikorsky
Stephen Gerard Siller
David Silver
Craig A. Silverstein
Nasima Hameed Simjee
Bruce Edward Simmons
Arthur Simon
Kenneth Alan Simon
Michael J. Simon
Paul Joseph Simon
Marianne Teresa Simone
Barry Simowitz
Jeff Lyal Simpson
Khamladai Singh
Kulwant Singh
Roshan Ramesh Singh
Thomas E. Sinton III
Peter A. Siracuse
Muriel Fay Siskopoulos
Joseph Michael Sisolak
John P. Skala
Francis Joseph Skidmore, Jr.
Toyena Skinner
Paul A. Skrzypek
Christopher Paul Slattery
Vincent Robert Slavin
Robert F. Sliwak
Paul K. Sloan
Stanley S. Smagala, Jr.
Wendy L. Small
Catherine Smith
Daniel Laurence Smith
George Eric Smith
James Gregory Smith
Jeffrey R. Smith
Joyce Patricia Smith
Karl T. Smith
Keisha Smith
Kevin Joseph Smith
Leon Smith, Jr.
Moira Ann Smith
Rosemary A. Smith
Bonnie Jeanne Smithwick
Rochelle Monique Snell
Leonard J. Snyder, Jr.
Astrid Elizabeth Sohan
Sushil S. Solanki
Ruben Solares
Naomi Leah Solomon
Daniel W. Song
Michael Charles Sorresse

Fabian Soto
Timothy Patrick Soulas
Gregory Spagnoletti
Donald F. Spampinato, Jr.
Thomas Sparacio
John Anthony Spataro
Robert W. Spear, Jr.
Maynard S. Spence, Jr.
George Edward Spencer III
Robert Andrew Spencer
Mary Rubina Sperando
Tina Spicer
Frank Spinelli
William E. Spitz
Joseph Spor, Jr.
Klaus Johannes Sprockamp
Saranya Srinuan
Fitzroy St. Rose
Michael F. Stabile
Lawrence T. Stack
Timothy M. Stackpole
Richard James Stadelberger
Eric Stahlman
Gregory Stajk
Alexandru Liviu Stan
Corina Stan
Mary Domenica Stanley
Anthony Starita
Jeffrey Stark
Derek James Statkevicus
Craig William Staub
William V. Steckman
Eric Thomas Steen
William R. Steiner
Alexander Steinman
Andrew Stergiopoulos
Andrew Stern
Martha Stevens
Michael James Stewart
Richard H. Stewart, Jr.
Sanford M. Stoller
Lonny Jay Stone
Jimmy Nevill Storey
Timothy Stout
Thomas Strada
James J. Straine, Jr.
Edward W. Straub
George J. Strauch, Jr.
Edward T. Strauss
Steven R. Strauss
Steven F. Strobert
Walwyn W. Stuart, Jr.
Benjamin Suarez
David Scott Suarez
Ramon Suarez
Yoichi Sugiyama
William Christopher Sugra
Daniel Suhr
David Marc Sullins
Christopher P. Sullivan
Patrick Sullivan
Thomas Sullivan
Hilario Soriano Sumaya, Jr.
James Joseph Suozzo

Colleen Supinski
Robert Sutcliffe
Seline Sutter
Claudia Suzette Sutton
John Francis Swaine
Kristine M. Swearson
Brian Edward Sweeney
Kenneth J. Swenson
Thomas Swift
Derek Ogilvie Sword
Kevin Thomas Szocik
Gina Sztejnberg
Norbert P. Szurkowski
Harry Taback
Joann Tabeek
Norma C. Taddei
Michael Taddonio
Keiichiro Takahashi
Keiji Takahashi
Phyllis Gail Talbot
Robert Talhami
Sean Patrick Tallon
Paul Talty
Maurita Tam
Rachel Tamares
Hector Tamayo
Michael Andrew Tamuccio
Kenichiro Tanaka
Rhondelle Cheri Tankard
Michael Anthony Tanner
Dennis Gerard Taormina, Jr.
Kenneth Joseph Tarantino
Allan Tarasiewicz
Ronald Tartaro
Darryl Anthony Taylor
Donnie Brooks Taylor
Lorisa Ceylon Taylor
Michael Morgan Taylor
Paul A. Tegtmeier
Yeshauant Tembe
Anthony Tempesta
Dorothy Pearl Temple
Stanley Temple
David Tengelin
Brian John Terrenzi
Lisa M. Terry
Shell Tester
Goumatie T. Thackurdeen
Sumati Thakur
Harshad Sham Thatte
Thomas F. Theurkauf, Jr.
Lesley Anne Thomas
Brian Thomas Thompson
Clive Thompson
Glenn Thompson
Nigel Bruce Thompson
Perry A. Thompson
Vanavah Alexei Thompson
William H. Thompson
Eric Raymond Thorpe
Nichola Angela Thorpe
Sal Edward Tieri, Jr.
John p Tierney
Mary Ellen Tiesi

William R. Tieste
Kenneth Francis Tietjen
Stephen Edward Tighe
Scott Charles Timmes
Michael E. Tinley
Jennifer M. Tino
Robert Frank Tipaldi
John James Tipping II
David Tirado
Hector Luis Tirado, Jr.
Michelle Lee Titolo
John J. Tobin
Richard Todisco
Vladimir Tomasevic
Stephen Kevin Tompsett
Thomas Tong
Doris Torres
Luis Eduardo Torres
Amy Elizabeth Toyen
Christopher Michael Traina
Daniel Patrick Trant
Abdoul Karim Traore
Glenn J. Travers
Walter Philip Travers
Felicia Y. Traylor-Bass
Lisa L. Trerotola
Karamo Trerra
Michael Angel Trinidad
Francis Joseph Trombino
Gregory James Trost
William P. Tselepis
Zhanetta Valentinovna Tsoy
Michael Tucker
Lance Richard Tumulty
Ching Ping Tung
Simon James Turner
Donald Joseph Tuzio
Robert T. Twomey
Jennifer Tzemis
John G. Ueltzhoeffer
Tyler V. Ugolyn
Michael A. Uliano
Jonathan J. Uman
Anil Shivhari Umarkar
Allen V. Upton
Diane Marie Urban
John Damien Vaccacio
Bradley Hodges Vadas
Renuta Vaidea
William Valcarcel
Felix Antonio Vale
Ivan Vale
Benito Valentin
Santos Valentin, Jr.
Carlton Francis Valvo II
Erica H. Van Acker
Kenneth W. Van Auken
Richard B. Van Hine
Daniel M. Van Laere
Edward Raymond Vanacore
Jon C. Vandevander
Barrett Vanvelzer, 4
Edward Vanvelzer
Paul Herman Vanvelzer

Frederick Thomas Varacchi
Gopalakrishnan Varadhan
David Vargas
Scott C. Vasel
Azael Ismael Vasquez
Arcangel Vazquez
Santos Vazquez
Peter Anthony Vega
Sankara S. Velamuri
Jorge Velazquez
Lawrence G. Veling
Anthony Mark Ventura
David Vera
Loretta Ann Vero
Christopher James Vialonga
Matthew Gilbert Vianna
Robert Anthony Vicario
Celeste Torres Victoria
Joanna Vidal
John T. Vigiano II
Joseph Vincent Vigiano
Frank J. Vignola, Jr.
Joseph Barry Vilardo
Sergio Villanueva
Chantal Vincelli
Melissa Vincent
Francine Ann Virgilio
Lawrence Virgilio
Joseph Gerard Visciano
Joshua S. Vitale
Maria Percoco Vola
Lynette D. Vosges
Garo H. Voskerijian
Alfred Vukosa
Gregory Kamal Bruno Wachtler
Gabriela Waisman
Courtney Wainsworth Walcott
Victor Wald
Benjamin James Walker
Glen Wall
Mitchel Scott Wallace
Peter Guyder Wallace
Robert Francis Wallace
Roy Michael Wallace
Jeanmarie Wallendorf
Matthew Blake Wallens
John Wallice, Jr.
Barbara P. Walsh
James Henry Walsh
Jeffrey P. Walz
Ching Wang
Weibin Wang
Michael Warchola
Stephen Gordon Ward
James Arthur Waring
Brian G. Warner
Derrick Washington
Charles Waters
James Thomas Waters, Jr.
Patrick J. Waters
Kenneth Thomas Watson
Michael Henry Waye
Todd Christopher Weaver
Walter Edward Weaver

Nathaniel Webb
Dinah Webster
Joanne Flora Weil
Michael T. Weinberg
Steven Weinberg
Scott Jeffrey Weingard
Steven George Weinstein
Simon Weiser
David M. Weiss
David Thomas Weiss
Vincent Michael Wells
Timothy Matthew Welty
Christian Hans Rudolf Wemmers
Ssu-Hui Wen
Oleh D. Wengerchuk
Peter M. West
Whitfield West, Jr.
Meredith Lynn Whalen
Eugene Whelan
Adam S. White
Edward James White III
James Patrick White
John Sylvester White
Kenneth Wilburn White, Jr.
Leonard Anthony White
Malissa Y. White
Wayne White
Leanne Marie Whiteside
Mark P. Whitford
Michael T. Wholey
Mary Catherine Wieman
Jeffrey David Wiener
Wilham J. Wik
Alison Marie Wildman
Glenn E. Wilkenson
John C. Willett
Brian Patrick Williams
Crossley Richard Williams, Jr.
David J. Williams
Deborah Lynn Williams
Kevin Michael Williams
Louie Anthony Williams
Louis Calvin Williams III
John P. Williamson
Donna Ann Wilson
William Wilson
David Harold Winton
Glenn J. Winuk
Thomas Francis Wise
Alan L. Wisniewski
Frank Thomas Wisniewski
David Wiswall
Sigrid Wiswe
Michael Wittenstein
Christopher W. Wodenshek
Martin P. Wohlforth
Katherine Susan Wolf
Jennifer Yen Wong
Siu Cheung Wong
Yin Ping Wong
Yuk Ping Wong
Brent James Woodall
James John Woods
Patrick J. Woods

Richard Herron Woodwell
David Terence Wooley
John Bentley Works
Martin Michael Wortley
Rodney James Wotton
William Wren
John Wayne Wright
Neil Robin Wright
Sandra Lee Wright
Jupiter Yambem
Suresh Yanamadala
Matthew David Yarnell
Myrna Yaskulka
Shakila Yasmin
Olabisi Shadie Layeni Yee
William Yemele
Edward P. York
Kevin Patrick York
Raymond R. York
Suzanne Youmans
Barrington Young
Jacqueline Young
Elkin Yuen
Joseph C. Zaccoli
Adel Agayby Zakhary
Arkady Zaltsman
Edwin J. Zambrana, Jr.
Robert Alan Zampieri
Mark Zangrilli
Ira Zaslow
Kenneth Albert Zelman
Abraham J. Zelmanowitz
Martin Morales Zempoaltecatl
Zhe Zeng
Marc Scott Zeplin
Jie Yao Justin Zhao
Ivelin Ziminski
Michael Joseph Zinzi
Charles A. Zion
Julie Lynne Zipper
Salvatore Zisa
Prokopios Paul Zois
Joseph J. Zuccala
Andrew S. Zucker
Igor Zukelman

American Airlines Flight 11 Victims

Anna Allison
David Lawrence Angell
Lynn Edwards Angell
Seima Aoyama
Barbara Jean Arestegui
Myra Joy Aronson
Christine Barbuto
Carolyn Beug
Kelly Ann Booms
Carol Marie Bouchard
Robin Lynne Kaplan
Neilie Anne Heffernan Casey
Jeffrey Dwayne Collman
Jeffrey W. Coombs
Tara Kathleen Creamer
Thelma Cuccinello

Patrick Currivan
Brian Paul Dale
David Dimeglio
Donald Americo Ditullio
Alberto Dominguez
Paige Marie Farley-Hackel
Alexander Milan Filipov
Carol Ann Flyzik
Paul J. Friedman
Karleton D.B. Fyfe
Peter Alan Gay
Linda M. George
Edmund Glazer
Lisa Reinhart Gordenstein
Andrew Peter Charles Curry Green
Peter Paul Hashem
Robert Jay Hayes
Edward R. Hennessy, Jr.
John A. Hofer
Cora Hidalgo Holland
John Nicholas Humber, Jr.
Waleed Joseph Iskandar
John Charles Jenkins
Charles Edward Jones
Barbara A. Keating
David P. Kovalcin
Judith Camilla Larocque
Natalie Janis Lasden
Daniel John Lee
Daniel M. Lewin
Sara Elizabeth Low
Susan A. Mackay
Karen Ann Martin
Thomas F. McGuinness, Jr.
Christopher D. Mello
Jeffrey Peter Mladenik
Carlos Alberto Montoya
Antonio Jesus Montoya Valdes
Laura Lee Morabito
Mildred Naiman
Laurie Ann Neira
Renee Lucille Newell
Kathleen Ann Nicosia
Jacqueline June Norton
Robert Grant Norton
John Ogonowski
Betty Ann Ong
Jane M. Orth
Thomas Nicholas Pecorelli
Berinthia B. Perkins
Sonia M. Puopolo
David E. Retik
Jean Destrehan Roger
Philip Martin Rosenzweig
Richard Barry Ross
Jessica Leigh Sachs
Rahma Salie
Heather Lee Smith
Dianne Bullis Snyder
Douglas Joel Stone
Xavier Suarez
Madeline Amy Sweeney
Michael Theodoridis
James Anthony Trentini

Mary Barbara Trentini
Pendyala Vamsikrishna
Mary Alice Wahlstrom
Kenneth Waldie
John Joseph Wenckus
Candace Lee Williams
Christopher Rudolph Zarba, Jr.

United Airlines Flight 175 Victims

Alona Abraham
Garnet Edward Bailey
Mark Lawrence Bavis
Graham Andrew Berkeley
Touri Bolourchi
Klaus Bothe
Daniel Raymond Brandhorst
David Reed Gamboa Brandhorst
John Brett Cahill
Christoffer Mikael Carstanjen
John J. Corcoran III
Dorothy Alma de Araujo
Ana Gloria Pocasangre Debarrera
Robert John Fangman
Lisa Anne Frost
Ronald Gamboa
Lynn Catherine Goodchild
Peter M. Goodrich
Douglas Alan Gowell
Francis Edward Grogan
Carl Max Hammond, Jr.
Christine Lee Hanson
Peter Burton Hanson
Susan Kim Hanson
Gerald Francis Hardacre
Eric Hartono
James Edward Hayden
Herbert Wilson Homer
Michael Robert Horrocks
Robert Adrien Jalbert
Amy N. Jarret
Ralph Kershaw
Heinrich Kimmig
Amy R. King
Brian Kinney
Kathryn L. LaBorie
Robert G. Leblanc
Maclovio Lopez, Jr.
Marianne Macfarlane
Alfred Gilles Marchand
Louis Mariani
Juliana McCourt
Ruth Magdaline McCourt
Wolfgang Peter Menzel
Shawn M. Nassaney
Marie Pappalardo
Patrick J. Quigley IV
Frederick Charles Rimmele III
James Roux
Jesus Sanchez
Victor J. Saracini
Mary Kathleen Shearer
Robert M. Shearer
Jane Louise Simpkin

Brian David Sweeney
Michael C. Tarrou
Alicia N. Titus
Timothy Ray Ward
William Michael Weems

Pentagon Victims
USA - United Stated Army

USN - United States Navy

SPC Craig S. Amundson, USA
YN3 Melissa Rose Barnes, USN
MSG Max J. Beilke, Retired
IT2 Kris Romeo Bishundat, USN
Carrie R. Blagburn
COL Canfield D. Boone, ARNG
Donna M. Bowen
Allen P. Boyle
ET3 Christopher L. Burford, USN
ET3 Daniel M. Caballero, USN
SFC Jose O. Calderon-Olmedo, USA
Angelene C. Carter
Sharon A. Carver
SFC John J. Chada, USA, Retired
Rosa Maria Chapa
Julian T. Cooper
LCDR Eric A. Cranford, USN
Ada M. Davis
CAPT Gerald F. DeConto, USN
LTC Jerry D. Dickerson, USA
IT1 Johnnie Doctor, Jr., USN
CAPT Robert E. Dolan, Jr., USN
CDR William H. Donovan, USN
CDR Patrick Dunn, USN
AG1 Edward T. Earhart, USN
LCDR Robert R. Elseth, USNR
SK3 Jamie L. Fallon, USN
Amelia V. Fields
Gerald P. Fisher
AG2 Matthew M. Flocco, USN
Sandra N. Foster
CAPT Lawrence D. Getzfred, USN
Cortez Ghee
Brenda C. Gibson
COL Ronald F. Golinski, USA, Retired
Diane Hale-McKinzy
Carolyn B. Halmon
Sheila M.S. Hein
ET1 Ronald J. Hemenway, USN
MAJ Wallace Cole Hogan, Jr., USA
SSG Jimmie I. Holley, USA, Retired
Angela M. Houtz
Brady Kay Howell
Peggie M. Hurt
LTC Stephen N. Hyland, Jr., USA
Lt Col Robert J. Hymel, USAF, Retired
SGM Lacey B. Ivory, USA
LTC Dennis M. Johnson, USA
Judith L. Jones
Brenda Kegler
LT Michael S. Lamana, USN
David W. Laychak
Samantha L. Lightbourn-Allen

MAJ Stephen V. Long, USA
James T. Lynch, Jr.
Terence M. Lynch
OS2 Nehamon Lyons IV, USN
Shelley A. Marshall
Teresa M. Martin
Ada L. Mason-Acker
LTC Dean E. Mattson, USA
LTG Timothy J. Maude, USA
Robert J. Maxwell
Molly L. McKenzie
Patricia E. Mickley
MAJ Ronald D. Milam, USA
Gerard P. Moran, Jr.
Odessa V. Morris
ET1 Brian A. Moss, USN
Teddington H. Moy
LCDR Patrick J. Murphy, USNR
Khang Ngoc Nguyen
DM2 Michael A. Noeth, USN
Ruben S. Ornedo
Diana B. Padro
LT Jonas M. Panik, USNR
MAJ Clifford L. Patterson, Jr., USA
LT Darin H. Pontell, USNR
Scott Powell
CAPT Jack D. Punches, USN, Retired
AW1 Joseph J. Pycior, Jr., USN
Deborah A. Ramsaur
Rhonda Sue Rasmussen
IT1 Marsha D. Ratchford, USN
Martha M. Reszke
Cecelia E. (Lawson) Richard
Edward V. Rowenhorst
Judy Rowlett
SGM Robert E. Russell, USA, Retired
CW4 William R. Ruth, ARNG
Charles E. Sabin, Sr.
Marjorie C. Salamone
COL David M. Scales, USA
CDR Robert A. Schlegel, USN
Janice M. Scott
LTC Michael L. Selves, USA, Retired
Marian H. Serva
CDR Dan F. Shanower, USN
Antionette M. Sherman
Diane M. Simmons
Cheryle D. Sincock
ITC Gregg H. Smallwood, USN
LTC Gary F. Smith, USA, Retired
Patricia J. Statz
Edna L. Stephens
SGM Larry L. Strickland, USA
LTC Kip P. Taylor, USA
Sandra C. Taylor
LTC Karl W. Teepe, USA, Retired
SGT Tamara C. Thurman, USA
LCDR Otis V. Tolbert, USN
SSG Willie Q. Troy, USA, Retired
LCDR Ronald J. Vauk, USNR

LTC Karen J. Wagner, USA
Meta L. (Fuller) Waller
SPC Chin Sun Pak Wells, USA
SSG Maudlyn A. White, USA
Sandra L. White
Ernest M. Willcher
LCDR David L. Williams, USN
MAJ Dwayne Williams, USA
RMC Marvin Roger Woods, USN, Retired
IT2 Kevin W. Yokum, USN
ITC Donald M. Young, USN
Edmond G. Young, Jr.
Lisa L. Young

American Airlines Flight 77 Victims

Paul W. Ambrose
Yeneneh Betru
Mary Jane Booth
Bernard C. Brown, II
CAPT Charles F. Burlingame III, USNR, Retired
Suzanne M. Calley
William E. Caswell
David M. Charlebois
Sarah M. Clark
Asia S. Cottom
James D. Debeuneure
Rodney Dickens
Eddie A. Dillard
LCDR Charles A. Droz III, USN, Retired
Barbara G. Edwards
Charles S. Falkenberg
Dana Falkenberg
Zoe Falkenberg
J. Joseph Ferguson
Darlene E. Flagg
RADM Wilson F. Flagg, USNR, Retired
1stLt Richard P. Gabriel, USMC, Retired
Ian J. Gray
Stanley R. Hall
Michele M. Heidenberger
Bryan C. Jack
Steven D. Jacoby
Ann C. Judge
Chandler R. Keller
Yvonne E. Kennedy
Norma Cruz Khan
Karen Ann Kincaid
Dong Chul Lee
Jennifer Lewis
Kenneth E. Lewis
Renee A. May
Dora Marie Menchaca
Christopher C. Newton
Barbara K. Olson
Ruben S. Ornedo
Robert Penninger
Robert R. Ploger III
Zandra F. Ploger

Lisa J. Raines
Todd H. Reuben
John P. Sammartino
George W. Simmons
Donald D. Simmons
Mari-Rae Sopper
Robert Speisman
Norma Lang Steuerle
Hilda E. Taylor
Leonard E. Taylor
Sandra D. Teague
Leslie A. Whittington
CAPT John D. Yamnicky, Sr., USN, Retired
Vicki Yancey
Shuyin Yang
Yuguag Zheng

United Airlines Flight 93 Victims

Christian Adams
Lorraine G. Bay
Todd Beamer
Alan Beaven
Mark K. Bingham
Deora Frances Bodley
Sandra W. Bradshaw
Marion Britton
Thomas E. Burnett Jr.
William Cashman
Georgine Rose Corrigan
Patricia Cushing
Jason Dahl
Joseph Deluca
Patrick Driscoll
Edward Porter Felt
Jane C. Folger
Colleen Fraser
Andrew Garcia
Jeremy Glick
Lauren Grandcolas
Wanda A. Green
Donald F. Greene
Linda Gronlund
Richard Guadagno
Leroy Homer, Jr.
Toshiya Kuge
CeeCee Lyles
Hilda Marcin
Waleska Martinez
Nicole Miller
Louis J. Nacke, II
Donald Arthur Peterson
Jean Hoadley Peterson
Mark Rothenberg
Christine Snyder
John Talignani
Honor Elizabeth Wainio
Deborah Ann Jacobs Welsh
Kristin Gould White

Sources

The 9/11 Commission Report, published 2004

Collier's Encyclopedia Volume 1, pp. 184-191 Copyright 1991 Macmillan Educational Company

The Columbia Encyclopedia as accessed through Yahoo.com

New World Encyclopedia http://www.newworldencyclopedia.org/entry/Info:Main_Page

Wikipedia www.wikipedia.org

Sheena Chi's wonderful Flickr stream of 9/11 memorial photos from all over the U.S. Her collection of 9/11 memorials is really the place to go on the Internet to see many of the country's tangible memories of that day. Where some towns don't even have pictures or information concerning their memorials on the Web, Sheena does. www.flickr.com/groups/sheenachi/

Voices of September 11th 9/11 Living Memorial
www.voicesofseptember11.org/dev/memorials.php?idtocitems=1,6,16

The National September 11 Memorial www.911memorial.org/

Empty Sky, The New Jersey September 11 Memorial http://nj911memorial.net/1901.html

Flight 93 National Memorial www.nps.gov/flni/index.htm

The Pentagon September 11 Memorial http://pentagonmemorial.org/

Fox News September 11 victim's list www.foxnews.com/story/0,2933,62151,00.html

Illustrations

Cover photo: Liberty State Park, Jersey City, New Jersey

Photo Credits

Smoking Towers, p. 15. The National September 11 Memorial Website

Damaged Pentagon, p. 16. National 9/11 Pentagon Memorial Website

Crash at Shanksville, p. 16. Flight 93 National Memorial Website

Ayatollah Khomeini, p. 19. conservapedia.com

Iran Embassy Storming, p. 19. conservapedia.com

Tomahawk Launch, p. 21. U.S. Navy photo by Lt.j.g. Monika Hess/Released

Rescue at the Pentagon, p. 22. U.S. Air Force photo by Staff Sgt. Gary Coppage

Tribute in Light, p. 24. U.S. Air Force photo/Denise Gould

INDEX

About the Authors

Brian Holmes graduated in 1985 from Northern Michigan University in the frigid Upper Peninsula of Michigan with a Bachelor of Science degree in English Creative Writing, with minors in Philosophy and Conservation. That summer he began working in the publishing industry by writing local sports for a penny shopper newspaper, and was paid in pennies for his time. Mr. Holmes has continued to work in publishing for more than twenty years, as a proofreader, copy editor, editor, and educational writer.

In the mid-1990s Brian published a widely distributed poetry journal called *The New Jersey Review of Literature,* acting as editor, publisher, marketer, and distributor. He also wrote a horror/adventure screenplay called *Homo Assassinatus*, which won Honorable Mention in the Filmmakers.com Screenplay Competition 2000, as well as an unproduced episode of *Highlander* the TV Series. Brian is an avid amateur photographer, history buff, political observer, and blogger. Besides his three blogs, (The Old Republic Gazette, Bigscreen Ballyhoo and Cash Saving Insider Strategies) Holmes has operated two or three websites as well, including ChooseYourPrez.com which extensively presented the candidates for the 2008 election, and GradeAedits.com, a professional editing website.

Min Xie is from the city of Guangzhou in Guangdong province, China and has resided in the U.S. since 2009. She is an artist, having taken classes in Hua Nan Art College. Xie is also adept at photography and photoediting and has more than ten years experience in consumer photo production and sales. Holmes and Xie have been married since 11/11/11 and live in Middlesex County, New Jersey.

For more information go to www.nj911memorials.com.

Made in the USA
Charleston, SC
24 August 2012